El Cid

El Cid

Philip Koslow

CHELSEA HOUSE PUBLISHERS
NEW YORK ■ PHILADELPHIA

CHELSEA HOUSE PUBLISHERS

Editorial Director: Richard Rennert
Executive Managing Editor: Karyn Gullen Browne
Executive Editor: Sean Dolan
Copy Chief: Philip Koslow
Picture Editor: Adrian G. Allen
Art Director: Nora Wertz
Manufacturing Director: Gerald Levine
Systems Manager: Lindsey Ottman
Production Coordinator: Marie Claire Cebrián-Ume

HISPANICS OF ACHIEVEMENT
Senior Editor: John W. Selfridge

Staff for *EL CID*
Copy Editor: Margaret Dornfeld
Designer: Robert Yaffe
Picture Researcher: Lisa Kirschner
Cover Illustration: Daniel O'Leary

3 5 7 9 8 6 4 2

Library of Congress Cataloging-in-Publication Data
Koslow, Philip.
El Cid/Philip Koslow.
p. cm.—(Hispanics of achievement)
Includes bibliographical references and index.
Summary: The life and adventures of the eleventh century military leader who be-
came one of Spain's national heroes.
ISBN 0-7910-1239-5
0-7910-1266-2 (pbk.)
1. Cid, ca. 1043–1099—Juvenile literature. 2. Spain—History—711–1516—Juvenile
literature. 3. Heroes—Spain—Biography—Juvenile literature. [1. Cid, ca. 1043–1099.
2. Heroes. 3. Spain—History—711–1516.]
DP103.7.C53K67 1993
CIP
946'.02'092—dc20
[B]
AC

CONTENTS

HISPANICS OF ACHIEVEMENT

JOAN BAEZ
Mexican-American folksinger

RUBÉN BLADES
Panamanian lawyer and entertainer

JORGE LUIS BORGES
Argentine writer

PABLO CASALS
Spanish cellist and conductor

MIGUEL DE CERVANTES
Spanish writer

CESAR CHAVEZ
Mexican-American labor leader

EL CID
Spanish military leader

ROBERTO CLEMENTE
Puerto Rican baseball player

SALVADOR DALÍ
Spanish painter

PLÁCIDO DOMINGO
Spanish singer

GLORIA ESTEFAN
Cuban-American singer

JULIO IGLESIAS
Spanish singer

RAUL JULIA
Puerto Rican actor

GABRIEL GARCÍA MÁRQUEZ
Colombian writer

FRANCISCO JOSÉ DE GOYA
Spanish painter

FRIDA KAHLO
Mexican painter

JOSÉ MARTÍ
Cuban revolutionary and poet

RITA MORENO
Puerto Rican singer and actress

PABLO NERUDA
Chilean poet and diplomat

ANTONIA NOVELLO
U.S. surgeon general

OCTAVIO PAZ
Mexican poet and critic

PABLO PICASSO
Spanish artist

ANTHONY QUINN
Mexican-American actor

DIEGO RIVERA
Mexican painter

LINDA RONSTADT
Mexican-American singer

ANTONIO LÓPEZ DE SANTA ANNA
Mexican general and politician

GEORGE SANTAYANA
Spanish philosopher and poet

JUNÍPERO SERRA
Spanish missionary and explorer

LEE TREVINO
Mexican-American golfer

DIEGO VELÁZQUEZ
Spanish painter

PANCHO VILLA
Mexican revolutionary

CHELSEA HOUSE PUBLISHERS

HISPANICS OF ACHIEVEMENT

Rodolfo Cardona

The Spanish language and many other elements of Spanish culture are present in the United States today and have been since the country's earliest beginnings. Some of these elements have come directly from the Iberian Peninsula; others have come indirectly, by way of Mexico, the Caribbean basin, and the countries of Central and South America.

Spanish culture has influenced America in many subtle ways, and consequently many Americans remain relatively unaware of the extent of its impact. The vast majority of them recognize the influence of Spanish culture in America, but they often do not realize the great importance and long history of that influence. This is partly because Americans have tended to judge the Hispanic influence in the United States in statistical terms rather than to look closely at the ways in which individual Hispanics have profoundly affected American culture. For this reason, it is fitting that Americans obtain more than a passing acquaintance with the origins of these Spanish cultural elements and gain an understanding of how they have been woven into the fabric of American society.

It is well documented that Spanish seafarers were the first to explore and colonize many of the early territories of what is today called the United States of America. For this reason, students of geography discover Hispanic names all over the map of the United States. For instance, the Strait of Juan de Fuca was named after the Spanish explorer who first navigated the waters of the Pacific Northwest; the names of states such as Arizona (arid zone), Montana (mountain), Florida (thus named because it was reached on Easter Sunday, which in Spanish is called the feast of Pascua Florida), and California (named after a fictitious land in one of the first and probably the most popular among the Spanish novels of chivalry, *Amadis of Gaul*) are all derived from Spanish; and there are numerous mountains, rivers, canyons, towns, and cities with Spanish names throughout the United States.

Not only explorers but many other illustrious figures in Spanish history have helped define American culture. For example, the 13th-century king of Spain, Alfonso X, also known as the Learned, may be unknown to the majority of Americans, but his work on the codification of Spanish law has greatly influenced the evolution of American law, particularly in the jurisdictions of the Southwest. For this contribution a statue of him stands in the rotunda of the Capitol in Washington, D.C. Likewise, the name Diego Rivera may be unfamiliar to most Americans, but this Mexican painter influenced many American artists whose paintings, commissioned during the Great Depression and the New Deal era of the 1930s, adorn the walls of government buildings throughout the United States. In recent years the contributions of Puerto Ricans, Mexicans, Mexican Americans (Chicanos), and Cubans in American cities such as Boston, Chicago, Los Angeles, Miami, Minneapolis, New York, and San Antonio have been enormous.

The importance of the Spanish language in this vast cultural complex cannot be overstated. Spanish, after all, is second only to English as the most widely spoken of Western languages within the United States as well as in the entire world. The popularity of the Spanish language in America has a long history.

In addition to Spanish exploration of the New World, the great Spanish literary tradition served as a vehicle for bringing the language and culture to America. Interest in Spanish literature in America began when English immigrants brought with them translations of Spanish masterpieces of the Golden Age. As early as 1683, private libraries in Philadelphia and Boston contained copies of the first picaresque novel, *Lazarillo de Tormes*, translations of Francisco de Quevedo's *Los Sueños*, and copies of the immortal epic of reality and illusion *Don Quixote*, by the great Spanish writer Miguel de Cervantes. It would not be surprising if Cotton Mather, the arch-Puritan, read *Don Quixote* in its original Spanish, if only to enrich his vocabulary in preparation for his writing *La fe del cristiano en 24 artículos de la Institución de Cristo, enviada a los españoles para que abran sus ojos* (The Christian's Faith in 24 Articles of the Institution of Christ, Sent to the Spaniards to Open Their Eyes), published in Boston in 1699.

Over the years, Spanish authors and their works have had a vast influence on American literature—from Washington Irving, John Steinbeck, and Ernest Hemingway in the novel to Henry Wadsworth Longfellow and Archibald MacLeish in poetry. Such important American writers as James Fenimore Cooper, Edgar Allan Poe, Walt Whitman, Mark Twain, and Herman Melville all owe a sizable debt to the Spanish literary tradition. Some writers, such as Willa Cather and Maxwell Anderson, who explored Spanish themes they came into contact with in the American Southwest and Mexico, were influenced less directly but no less profoundly.

Important contributions to a knowledge of Spanish culture in the United States were also made by many lesser known individuals—teachers, publishers, historians, entrepreneurs, and others—with a love for Spanish culture. One of the most significant of these contributions was made by Abiel Smith, a Harvard College graduate of the class of 1764, when he bequeathed stock worth $20,000 to Harvard for the support of a professor of French and Spanish. By 1819 this endowment had produced enough income to appoint a professor, and the philologist and humanist George Ticknor became the first holder of the Abiel

Smith Chair, which was the very first endowed Chair at Harvard University. Other illustrious holders of the Smith Chair would include the poets Henry Wadsworth Longfellow and James Russell Lowell.

A highly respected teacher and scholar, Ticknor was also a collector of Spanish books, and as such he made a very special contribution to America's knowledge of Spanish culture. He was instrumental in amassing for Harvard libraries one of the first and most impressive collections of Spanish books in the United States. He also had a valuable personal collection of Spanish books and manuscripts, which he bequeathed to the Boston Public Library.

With the creation of the Abiel Smith Chair, Spanish language and literature courses became part of the curriculum at Harvard, which also went on to become the first American university to offer graduate studies in Romance languages. Other colleges and universities throughout the United States gradually followed Harvard's example, and today Spanish language and culture may be studied at most American institutions of higher learning.

No discussion of the Spanish influence in the United States, however brief, would be complete without a mention of the Spanish influence on art. Important American artists such as John Singer Sargent, James A. M. Whistler, Thomas Eakins, and Mary Cassatt all explored Spanish subjects and experimented with Spanish techniques. Virtually every serious American artist living today has studied the work of the Spanish masters as well as the great 20th-century Spanish painters Salvador Dalí, Joan Miró, and Pablo Picasso.

The most pervasive Spanish influence in America, however, has probably been in music. Compositions such as Leonard Bernstein's *West Side Story*, the Latinization of William Shakespeare's *Romeo and Juliet* set in New York's Puerto Rican quarter, and Aaron Copland's *Salon Mexico* are two obvious examples. In general, one can hear the influence of Latin rhythms—from tango to mambo, from guaracha to salsa—in virtually every form of American music.

This series of biographies, which Chelsea House has published under the general title HISPANICS OF ACHIEVEMENT, constitutes further recognition of—and a renewed effort to bring forth to the consciousness of America's young people—the contributions that Hispanic people have made not only in the United States but throughout the civilized world. The men and women who are featured in this series have attained a high level of accomplishment in their respective fields of endeavor and have made a permanent mark on American society.

The title of this series must be understood in its broadest possible sense: The term *Hispanics* is intended to include Spaniards, Spanish Americans, and individuals from many countries whose language and culture have either direct or indirect Spanish origins. The names of many of the people included in this series will be immediately familiar; others will be less recognizable. All, however, have attained recognition within their own countries, and often their fame has transcended their borders.

The series HISPANICS OF ACHIEVEMENT thus addresses the attainments and struggles of Hispanic people in the United States and seeks to tell the stories of individuals whose personal and professional lives in some way reflect the larger Hispanic experience. These stories are exemplary of what human beings can accomplish, often against daunting odds and by extraordinary personal sacrifice, where there is conviction and determination. Fray Junípero Serra, the 18th-century Spanish Franciscan missionary, is one such individual. Although in very poor health, he devoted the last 15 years of his life to the foundation of missions throughout California—then a mostly unsettled expanse of land—in an effort to bring a better life to Native Americans through the cultivation of crafts and animal husbandry. An example from recent times, the Mexican-American labor leader Cesar Chavez has battled bitter opposition and made untold personal sacrifices in his effort to help poor agricultural workers who have been exploited for decades on farms throughout the Southwest.

The talent with which each one of these men and women may have been endowed required dedication and hard work to develop and become fully realized. Many of them have enjoyed rewards for their efforts during their own lifetime, whereas others have died poor and unrecognized. For some it took a long time to achieve their goals, for others success came at an early age, and for still others the struggle continues. All of them, however, stand out as people whose lives have made a difference, whose achievements we need to recognize today and should continue to honor in the future.

El Cid

"SANTIAGO!"

In late October 1094, an invading army surrounded the Spanish city of Valencia. Day and night, the residents of the city heard the din of thousands of drums outside the walls. The landscape was dominated by the invaders' tents, and the air was filled with their wailing war cries. Valencia's defenders, though bolstered by their leader, the renowned warrior Rodrigo Díaz, were hopelessly outnumbered. It was only a matter of time before the invaders closed in for the kill.

This was not the first time that Valencia, located on the eastern coast of Spain, had faced the onslaught of a conquering army. For three centuries, the Iberian Peninsula, which today comprises the nations of Spain and Portugal, was a province of the mighty Roman Empire. Valencia was established as a military camp by the Romans around 139 B.C. It was sacked in 75 B.C. during one of Rome's civil wars and then rebuilt as a full-fledged Roman colony, known as Valentia Edetanorum. After the fall of the Roman Empire during the 5th century A.D., the city fell to the Visigoths, a warlike people who swept into the peninsula from central Europe. Valencia remained a Visigothic city until 714,

The 11th-century Castilian soldier of fortune Rodrigo Díaz, known as El Cid, began his career in the service of the Christian kings of Castile. In 1081, banished by King Alfonso VI, he set off on a life of exploits that would make him a national hero.

15

when a new group of conquerors entered its gates. This time the invaders came not from the north but from the hot desert lands across the Mediterranean. They were Moors from Africa.

Unlike the Visigoths, who had followed the majority of European peoples in adopting Christianity, the Moors were Muslims. They practiced the religion of Islam, established by the prophet Muhammad in the deserts of Arabia during the 7th century. By the time of his death in 632, Muhammad had gained a mass of devoted followers who were eager to spread the faith: they did so by conquering all the territory that constitutes the present-day Middle East. Toward the end of the 7th century, the Muslim Arabs extended their domain to the former Roman provinces in North Africa, which were populated by a people known as the Berbers.

The Berbers quickly adopted both the religion and the warlike fire of their conquerors. In 711, an army of Moors—as the combination of Berbers and Arabs became known—crossed the narrow expanse of the Mediterranean Sea between Morocco and Gibraltar. The operation was intended as an exploratory raid, designed to test the strength of the Visigothic armies. The Visigoths, however, had been fighting in the north and were not prepared to meet a challenge from across the sea. Their king, Roderick, quickly assembled an inexperienced army and hurried south to meet the Moors near the Guadalquivir River. In the ensuing battle, the Visigoths were routed, and Roderick was killed.

The death of Roderick left a power vacuum on the Iberian Peninsula, and the Moors were quick to grasp the opportunity. By 720 they had conquered all but the northernmost portions of the peninsula and had established a flourishing civilization that was not to be fully dislodged until 1492. In 1012, Valencia was made the capital of an independent Moorish kingdom that prospered until 1093, when it was conquered by Rodrigo Díaz, known to history as El Cid.

The title El Cid derived from the Arabic word *sayyid*, which means "lord." Historians are not certain whether Rodrigo was known as El Cid during his lifetime or whether the title was first used by those who wrote of him after his death. However, there is no doubt that well before he conquered Valencia he was a warrior of legendary stature, feared and celebrated throughout Spain.

Rodrigo had begun his career in the service of the kings of Castile, Spain's most powerful Christian realm. However, his relations with King Alfonso VI, who ascended the throne in 1072, were often stormy. Rodrigo's success earned him enemies at Alfonso's court, and these men continually questioned his loyalty. When King Alfonso finally banished Rodrigo in 1081, the renowned knight quickly became a power in his own right. Leading his own private army, he took what he needed from Christians and Muslims alike. By 1093, he was the master of Spain's entire southeastern coast. The only threat to his power came from a group of militant Muslims from North Africa, the Almoravids, who were sweeping through southern Spain and threatening to overrun the entire peninsula.

In 1094, Rodrigo captured Valencia before it could fall into the hands of the Almoravids. Once he was in possession of the city, however, he was himself subject to attack. Yusuf ibn Tashufin, the leader of the Almoravids, had never been defeated in battle, and by late October his army had encamped at Cuarte, a broad plain just to the west of Valencia. El Cid was now a captive within his own domain.

The exact strength of Yusuf's army is uncertain. The *Poema de Mío Cid*, the great Spanish epic poem written about a century after Rodrigo's death, claims that the Almoravids numbered 50,000. The renowned Spanish historian Ramón Menéndez Pidal, whose 1929 book *La España del Cid* (The Cid and His Spain) was for many years the primary source, adopted the figure of 150,000 from an 11th-century narrative known as the *Historia Roderici*. Later historians, while recognizing the value of Menéndez Pidal's narrative, have questioned some of the facts he adopted from the medieval sources. Most notably, the British historian Richard Fletcher reexamined all the available evidence during the 1980s; in his book *The Quest for El Cid*, published in 1989, he asserted that the Al-

A relief depicting a warrior on horseback. In 1094, El Cid and his army captured the Moorish kingdom of Valencia, but soon the territory was surrounded by Almoravids, a group of militant Muslims from North Africa, and El Cid became a captive within the confines of his own realm.

moravids could not have numbered much more than 25,000.

In any case, Rodrigo and his band of knights, an army of perhaps 4,000 in all, were badly outnumbered. The only advantage they possessed lay in the quality of their armor. Although European knights had not yet adopted the elaborate suits of plate armor that came into use after the 14th century, they were well protected in combat by coats of mail. Mail was made by riveting hundreds of small metal rings together until they formed a continuous fabric that was flexible enough to permit movement while protecting the body. The mail was fashioned into long shirts with wide, open sleeves and also into leggings and hoods. In addition to their mail hoods, knights also wore iron helmets with long nose guards. Many knights wore padded shirts beneath their mail, in order to prevent bruises from sword blows. Shields were usually long and triangular, made of wood reinforced with iron. The principal weapons of attack were the lance and the broadsword.

The Muslims, on the other hand, fought with scarcely any protection. Illustrated medieval manuscripts depict them in cloth tunics and turbans, without any visible armor. They carried lances, light swords, and small, round shields made of rhinoceros hide. Lacking the armament and skill in combat enjoyed by their European opponents, the Almoravids had won their victories through clever tactics and psychological warfare. The thunderous beating of their drums, their wailing cries, and their shouts of "Muhammad!" were terrifying to Europeans, who had never heard such things in battle.

In addition, the Muslims employed unique strategies on the battlefield. Rather than seeking to engage in one-on-one combat as the Europeans did, the Almoravids—like commanders of a later day—trained their soldiers to move in groups according to specific commands, so that they could attack in a body. To further harass the enemy, archers arranged in parallel rows unleashed showers of arrows—a technique scorned by Europeans until the Battle of Crécy in 1346, when it helped the English defeat a vastly superior French force. Such tactics had led the Almoravids to a decisive victory over King Alfonso at the Battle of Sagrajas in 1086. By the fall of 1094, it appeared as though the Almoravids could have as much of Spain as they desired.

El Cid believed otherwise. According to the *Poema de Mío Cid*, he had recently brought his wife, Doña Jimena, and his daughters, Cristina and María, to Valencia from Castile, where they had remained during his exile. When the Almoravids encamped outside the city walls and began to beat their drums, the women were understandably frightened. The poet recounts that El Cid merely stroked his flowing beard, which he had not trimmed ever since King Alfonso had banished him and which, he liked to boast, had never been plucked by any man in Spain.

"Noble wife," he told Doña Jimena, "do not be alarmed. This is great and wonderful wealth that is coming to us. You have no sooner arrived than they wish to give you a present. Your daughters are of marriageable age and they come with a dowry for them." He vowed that within two weeks he would place the drums before his wife and then give them to the bishop, who would hang them in the church as a tribute to the Virgin Mary.

For 10 days—in the account of Menéndez Pidal—the Almoravids besieged Valencia, riding boldly up to the city walls and letting out deafening yells, while the archers showered arrows on the roofs of the houses. Rodrigo's strategy, clearly, was to hang back as

Moors in battle. The Almoravids moved to take Valencia from El Cid, who for 10 days held his forces back, hoping to lull his attackers into a state of overconfidence. Then his army retaliated and routed the Almoravids.

long as possible, and so lull the enemy into a state of overconfidence. When he decided that the time was right, he roused his knights at three o'clock in the morning and assembled them in the church. After saying mass, Bishop Jerónimo declared to the soldiers, "I absolve from sin all those who die with their faces to the enemy; God will receive their souls." Just before sunrise, El Cid mounted his horse, Babieca, and rode out at the head of his 4,000 knights, prepared to meet Yusuf and the Almoravids.

The exact strategy employed by Rodrigo on the plains of Cuarte was never recorded in great detail. Fletcher, following Arabic sources, concludes that he divided his forces into two parts and used one to lure the Almoravids into a trap. It may safely be supposed that in the face of such superior numbers he chose his battleground carefully, much as King Henry V of England did at Agincourt in 1415, when he defeated a huge assemblage of mounted French knights with a small band of foot soldiers. The classic tactic in such a case, as explained by historian John Keegan in his book *The Face of Battle*, would be to draw the enemy into an area that was bounded on both sides by trees or other obstacles. In such an area, the opponent would be unable to spread out; only his front ranks would be able to engage in fighting, thus evening the odds.

Conceivably, Rodrigo's apparent unwillingness to fight during the 10-day siege convinced the Almoravids that he was already a beaten man. Feeling certain of victory, they were more prone to concentrate their forces and pursue Rodrigo until he had led them to ground that suited his purpose. When this had happened, his 4,000 knights wheeled around, and with cries of "Santiago!"—the Spanish name of Saint James the Great, Spain's patron saint—they spurred their horses to the attack.

According to Menéndez Pidal, the knights of that time bent low over their saddle bows and charged with lowered lances. As soon as they had penetrated the enemy's lines, they executed a maneuver known as the *tornada*, wheeling quickly about and mounting a second charge before their opponents could regroup. At the same time, according to the *Poema de Mío Cid*, Rodrigo's number one lieutenant, Alvar Fáñez, came

A battle scene from an 11th-century Spanish Bible. Following the defeat of the Almoravids at Valencia, El Cid was known throughout Spain as a shrewd leader and valiant warrior.

around from the flank with a picked force of 130 knights and attacked the Almoravids from the rear. In a confined space, such a double assault—combined with superior armor, swordsmanship, and horsemanship—could be truly devastating. Before long, the Almoravids surrendered by the thousands while Yusuf, their commander, fled to safety inside his fortress at nearby Cullera. El Cid, whom the *Poema* describes as plying his sword in the battle until "the blood dripped down to his elbow," watched with satisfaction as his men stripped the Almoravid camp of money and valuables.

The Muslims were to remain in Spain for another 300 years, but El Cid's victory at Cuarte became enshrined in Spanish history as the beginning of the Reconquista (Reconquest). "The fame of this great victory spread to the neighboring kingdoms," wrote Menéndez Pidal, "and throughout the following year Christian notaries . . . dated their deeds by this event. A document of Aragon, for example, records, half in Latin and half in the Aragonese dialect, that 'This charter was made in the year that the Almoravids came to Valencia, when Roderic Didaç drove them out and captured all their *mehalla* [army].' "

During the ensuing centuries, the real-life Rodrigo Díaz was in many ways eclipsed by the legend of El Cid, the national hero of Spain, the devoted servant of his king, and the champion of Christianity. In modern times, however, the mystified El Cid has, along with many other legendary figures, undergone damaging scrutiny. Recent scholars have recognized that Rodrigo Díaz was one of many medieval warriors who were essentially soldiers of fortune, eager to enrich themselves and often willing to serve any master who promised them a good financial reward. It is a documented fact, for example, that during his exile Rodrigo spent several years in the service of the Muslim king of Zaragoza. There is also evidence to support the more romantic view of his nature. It is reasonable to conclude that Rodrigo was no less complex a character than other great historical figures. In order to come to terms with him, one must understand the tumultuous world in which he performed his deeds.

F. LIX

THE CRESCENT AND THE CROSS

Phoenician ships at sea in a violent storm. During the 8th century B.C., the Phoenicians sailed to and settled the south of the Iberian Peninsula, then home to a patchwork of nationalities.

By its very location, the land that eventually became Spain was destined to be a battleground. As S. J. Keay has expressed it in *Roman Britain*: "Iberia is the largest peninsula . . . in Europe and comprises many geographically distinct areas; it also occupies a unique position separating the Atlantic from the Mediterranean and Europe from Africa. This explains why Iberia has always been a country of passage, contact and confrontation between invaders and native peoples."

Human habitation in the peninsula has been traced back as far as 300,000 years. Some of the peoples who settled in Iberia were Celts from the north; others came from North Africa; still others came from the heartland of Europe across the Pyrenees Mountains. Over time, these peoples developed a variety of different cultures. By 1000 B.C. Iberia was home to a patchwork quilt of nationalities, many of whom gave their names to regions of present-day Spain: Cantabri, Callaici, Vascones, and Astures in the north; Lusitani in the west; Ilergaones and Contestani in the east; Oretani in the south.

At the same time, Iberia drew the interest of
seagoing explorers and merchants from the East.
Sometime during the 8th century B.C., the Phoenicians sailed from the eastern edge of the Mediterranean and established a settlement in the south of the
peninsula, near present-day Cádiz. Two centuries later,
they were followed by Greek traders, who installed
themselves farther up the eastern coast. The remains of
one Greek town, Emporion, are still well preserved
near the city of Gerona.

Iberia was drawn onto the stage of world history
during the 3rd century B.C., as a result of the struggle
between Rome and Carthage, a powerful city-state
on the coast of North Africa. During the First Punic
War (264–241), the Romans drove the Carthaginians
from Sicily, Corsica, and Sardinia, their island colonies
in the Mediterranean. To compensate for these losses,
the Carthaginians resolved to expand into Iberia.
Under their great general Hannibal, who later led an
army across the Alps to attack Rome itself, the Carthaginians established a base at New Carthage (now
Cartagena) on the southeast coast of Iberia in 227. The
city of Saguntum (now Sagunto), farther up the coast,
became legendary in Spanish history for the resistance
of its people to the Carthaginians' siege in 219. The
city held out for more than a year, resisting both
threats and peace terms, before the superior forces of
the Carthaginians overwhelmed it. The Roman historian Livy described the defiant spirit of the Sagun-
tans: "Launching a full-scale assault he [Hannibal]
overwhelmed the town, having issued orders that no
man of military age should be spared. It was a bar-
barous order, though hardly avoidable, as the event
proved; for how was it possible to show mercy to men
who in desperation either fought to the death or set
fire to their own houses and burned themselves alive
together with their wives and children?"

Hannibal crossing the Alps. During the 3rd century B.C., the Iberian Peninsula was drawn into a struggle for power between Rome and Carthage. The leader of the Carthaginian forces against Rome in the Second Punic War (218–201 B.C.), Hannibal is widely regarded as the greatest general of antiquity.

After Hannibal's daring invasion of Italy bogged down at the gates of Rome, the Romans counterattacked in Spain. In 209, a force of 21,000 Roman troops under Scipio Africanus overwhelmed New Carthage and ended the Carthaginians' bid to supplant Rome as the dominant power in the Mediterranean.

As a full-fledged province of the Roman Empire, the Iberian Peninsula became known as Hispania. Hispania prospered under Roman rule for four centuries, gaining a reputation for its rich silver mines, its abundant crops of corn, its excellent wines, and its spirited horses. Two of the more renowned Roman emperors, Trajan and Hadrian, were of Spanish origin; during the 1st century A.D., one-fourth of the members of the Roman Senate were Hispano-Romans. Apart from the names they bestowed on numerous regions and towns of the country, the Romans are remembered most in present-day Spain for their splendid works of architecture and engineering. They filled Hispania with mansions, tombs, temples, theaters, baths, bridges, and aqueducts. Many of these structures survive today: notable among them are the bridge over the river Tagus near Cáceres; the theater at Mérida; the lighthouse at La Coruña (now enclosed by a later structure); and the magnificent aqueduct whose 119 arches form a gateway to the city of Segovia.

For all the splendor of their rule, however, the Romans could not hold Hispania forever. In the winter of 406, a confederation of barbarian tribes from central Europe crossed the frozen Rhine River and invaded the Roman Empire. The Romans no longer had the strength to stop them, and the barbarians forged westward across Europe, carving up the Empire into territories that formed the basis of present-day France and Germany. On either September 28 or October 13, 409, the barbarians crossed the Pyrenees and entered Hispania.

Within two years, the peninsula was basically divided among four major groups—the Siling Vandals, the Alans, the Hasding Vandals, and the Suevis. However, the Romans had not given up. They forged an alliance with the Visigoths, who had settled in present-

A carved sarcophagus depicting a clash between Romans and barbarians. In 406, barbarian tribes from central Europe invaded the Roman Empire; three years later they crossed the Pyrenees and entered Hispania.

day France after sacking Rome, and the Visigoths invaded Spain on behalf of Rome in 416. After the Visigoths drove out their fellow barbarians, the Romans persuaded them to withdraw to their home territory. Forty years later, under their king Theodoric II, the Visigoths returned to Spain, this time for good. Establishing Seville as their capital, they proceeded during the 5th and 6th centuries to solidify their rule. In his book *Early Medieval Spain*, Roger Collins explains that the change of masters in Spain was not always uncomfortable for the country's residents: "In place of the universal dominion of the [Roman] emperor, Germanic kings and their followers, partly by force and partly by agreements, set up realms having a rough correspondence to the military divisions of the former Empire. . . . Although the process of transition was at times and in places violent and destructive, reactions to it were generally limited and localized, and more often marked by co-operation between the Roman provincials and their new masters, than by resistance."

Religion played a major role in the Visigoths' efforts to unify Iberia under the rule of their kings. During most of their history, the Visigoths had clung to the pagan religions of the Germanic tribes. That is, they worshiped a variety of gods, most of them representing forces of nature; in this they were quite similar to the Romans, who had been pagans throughout their early history. By the time the Visigoths pushed into western Europe, the Romans had adopted Christianity. The Visigoths and other tribes began to persecute Christians where they could, just as the Romans had previously done. In the end, the Visigoths proved equally unable to resist the appeal of the new religion. Their reasons for conversion may have been as much political as spiritual. The former Roman colonists were still the majority in Spain; by adopting the Latin language and the Christian religion, the Visigoths certainly made themselves far more acceptable to the people they meant to rule.

Whatever the motive behind it, the official adoption of Christianity during the reign of King Recared I (586–601) had far-reaching effects on Spanish history. Due to the unsettled conditions in the country, the monarchy and the church grew extremely close. The kings needed the sanction of the clergy to legitimize their rule, and the clergy felt that a strong state could promote their own desire for law and order. For this reason, the Spanish bishops began the ceremony of anointing the Visigothic kings with holy oil as they took possession of the throne, a practice that soon became standard in medieval and modern Europe. In addition, the bishops often excommunicated (expelled from the church) all those who rebelled against the king. In return, the kings protected and supported the church and funded the monasteries that were the only source of Christian culture in the era that became known as the Dark Ages.

The Visigoths invade Spain. During the 5th and 6th centuries, the Visigoths solidified their rule over the country. They established the city of Seville as their capital and attempted to unify Iberia under the rule of Christian kings.

A representation of nine Visigothic rulers and officials. After three centuries of rule, the Visigoths were replaced as the rulers of Spain by Muslim caliphs and emirs.

Even with the bonds of common language and religion, Spain did not enjoy stable leadership during the three centuries of Visigothic rule. If the Roman colonists were prone to accept the rule of the barbarian tribes, other peoples in Spain were not. The Visigothic kings often found themselves at war in the northern regions, trying to subdue the Suevi and the Basques, an ancient people whose origins have never been determined by scholars and whose desire for independence continues to the present day. At the same time, the Visigoths were plagued by internal conflicts, as various groups and families vied for control of the monarchy. Revolts were a continual threat, and those who sought the crown were prone to slaughter everyone who stood in their way—the king, his heirs, and all other potential rivals along with their families. The kings themselves often set the example for this sort of savagery by executing would-be rebels and confiscating their properties. Writing of King Chindesuinth (642–53), the bishop of Toledo, Eugenius II, described the late monarch as "ever the friend of evil deeds; committer of crimes . . . impious, obscene, infamous, ugly and wicked; not seeking the best, valuing the worst."

If such qualities were typical of the Visigothic rulers, it should not be surprising that in 711 a relatively small raiding force of North African Muslims was able to defeat a Visigothic army and then sweep rapidly northward to capture such cities as Toledo, Zaragoza, and León. By 715, Muslim caliphs and emirs had replaced the Visigothic kings as the masters of Spain.

Spain, with its racial and cultural mixture and its long history of upheaval, was not an easy territory to pacify. As early as 718, a Visigothic noble named Pelagius led a revolt against the Muslims in the north. Rather than try to crush the rebellion, the Muslims consented to the formation of Asturias, an independent Christian kingdom. To explain this apparent act of tolerance, historians have pointed out that the Muslims' method of warfare, relying on carefully synchronized troop movement, was unsuited to the mountainous terrain of the north. For this reason, they chose to fall back to armed frontiers farther south and make raids into the north when they felt there was loot to be gained from the northern kingdoms.

This was a wise decision, but their failure to secure the whole of Iberia may have set the stage for the eventual expulsion of the Muslims from the peninsula.

The Muslims' state, known as al-Andalus, was governed between 756 and 1031 by the Umayyad dynasty, who made their capital in the city of Córdoba, near the center of the peninsula. Al-Andalus emerged as one of the most important countries in Europe, but it was never an easy territory to govern. The racial and religious diversity of the country stood in the way of any real unity among the Umayyads' subjects. Hence the Umayyads were forced to give power to local leaders in the various regions of al-Andalus, and those leaders were as likely as the Visigothic nobles to rebel against control from the center.

The Umayyads put down revolts with extreme brutality. On November 16, 806, for example, known as the Day of the Ditch, 5,000 rebellious citizens of Toledo, one of the important cities of al-Andalus, were invited to a banquet by the city governor. Once assembled, they were slaughtered, on the orders of the emir al-Hakem I. (Their bodies were thrown into a ditch rather than given a formal burial.)

Considering the bloodshed caused by religious disputes throughout history, it might be assumed that al-Andalus was a dangerous place in which to be a non-Muslim. In fact, the Muslim rulers of Spain showed far more religious tolerance than the Christian regimes that preceded and followed them. Their treatment of Spain's Jewish population clearly illustrates their attitude. The Jews, who had scattered throughout the West after the Romans conquered Palestine, their original homeland, had not fared well at the hands of the Visigoths. From 506 on, the Jews of Hispania had been subject to a variety of laws banning them from marrying Christians, holding public office, or building new places of worship. Often at the urging of the church, Visigothic kings took increasingly harsh anti-Jewish measures. King Reccesuinth outlawed all Jewish religious practices, and King Chintila declared flatly that he did not want non-Catholics in his realm. On the whole, historians have found no evidence of popular feeling against the Jews or physical persecution of the sort that became common in Europe during later centuries. Many edicts, such as King Egica's decree in 694 that Jews be deprived of their property and pressed into slavery, were most likely never put into practice. But the Jews could not have felt they had much to lose from a change in rulers.

Although the Muslims had been known to spread their religion by the sword, their aggressive behavior was generally limited to those who practiced the various forms of paganism once common to the Middle East. They had a different attitude toward those who believed in a single god and were "people of the book," even when that god was Jehovah rather than the Muslims' Allah and the book was the Old Testament rather than the Koran. In al-Andalus, the Umayyads made no attempt to restrict Jewish worship or to bar Jews from public office. Indeed, under Muslim rule Spain became a center of Jewish learning.

One of the central figures in this process was Hasdai ibn Shaprut, who served as the personal physician to the caliph Abd-al-Rahman III during the latter part of the 10th century. Hasdai gained renown for his cure of King Sancho I of León, known as Sancho the Fat. King Sancho was ousted from power by Ordoño the Bad in 957, after he had become so obese that he could no longer mount a horse. Sancho sought the protection of Abd-al-Rahman, who put the deposed king under the care of Hasdai. By 960, a slimmed-down Sancho was back on his throne.

Beyond these medical duties, Hasdai became one of the leading figures in the caliph's court, often traveling through Europe on diplomatic missions. He used his influence to benefit the Jewish community in Córdoba, paying special attention to scholars. During the 10th century, Córdoba became a center for Jewish poetry, philosophy, and religious commentaries. The Jews showed their acceptance of their new masters by replacing Latin with Arabic as their everyday language, while Hebrew was reserved for religious studies.

The Muslims showed equal toleration toward Christians, especially in the countryside. However, their liberalism sometimes had a price. For example, Roger Collins cites a treaty between one of the emirs and a local Gothic lord in which Christians are granted freedom of religion in return for a yearly tribute of oil, honey, vinegar, and cash. In the large cities, the Muslims tended to be more strict. In Córdoba, for example, they forced the Christians to move their main church to another location so that a mosque could be built on the site, and they imposed a general ban on the ringing of church bells and the erection of new churches. Beyond these restrictions, there was no active repression of Christian worship.

Like the Jews of al-Andalus, Christians were allowed to serve as government officials. Christian officials were, however, well advised to convert to Islam if they wished to reach the higher levels of government. There are no exact figures available on the subject of conversion, but it is widely accepted that many Christians converted to Islam as a matter of convenience and then converted back to Christianity at a later date. Christian men were also obliged to convert if they wished to marry Muslim women. The law permitted mixed marriages only between Muslim men and Christian women, though the authorities were quite liberal about the religious upbringing of the children: the girls usually adopted Islam, and the boys adopted the Christian religion of their mother.

Not all Christians accommodated themselves to Muslim rule. Although Christianity had advanced by persuasion rather than force, the persecution of the early church by the Romans had made the church a tenacious and militant organization, determined to prevail over its enemies. By the 11th century, Christian knights would be sailing to Palestine to dislodge the Muslims from Jerusalem, the holy city of Christendom. In the meanwhile, opposition took more subtle forms. In the middle of the 9th century, there arose in Córdoba a phenomenon that became known as the martyr movement. The movement began when a Christian monk named Perfectus had an argument with some Muslims and loudly denounced their religion. A Muslim who overheard this argument reported Perfectus to a *qadi*, or Muslim judge. The qadi summoned Perfectus, quite prepared to accept an apology from the monk and dismiss the case. Perfectus, however, repeated his abuse of Islam to the qadi's face, leaving the qadi with no choice but to impose the sentence of death.

Following the example of Perfectus, a number of Christians, many of them monks, deliberately martyred themselves by denouncing Islam in public and effectively forcing the authorities to execute them. Fortunately for the tranquility of al-Andalus, the martyr movement was condemned by the Catholic church and never became widespread: records indicate that only 30 Christians were executed between 851 and 856. However, the willingness of Christians to die for their religious faith was a portent of the zeal that led them to persecute both Jews and Muslims in later centuries.

At the other end of the spectrum of Christian response to Muslim domination were the so-called Mozarabs. The Mozarabs were Christians who retained their religion but adopted Muslim culture,

which they spread throughout the Christian kingdoms as they migrated northward during the 9th and
10th centuries. There was a great need for this culture,
because the fall of the Roman Empire had also
brought about the end of Greek and Latin literature
and scholarship. Under the various barbarian kings,
Europe became an intellectual wasteland where the
monasteries supplied the only spark of learning. The
continent's gradual awakening from the Dark Ages is
due in large part to the influence of al-Andalus.

Because they were deeply imbued with the ancient scholarly traditions of the Middle East, Spain's
Muslim rulers vigorously supported the arts and
sciences. Equally important, the Muslims believed that
learning should not be restricted to a small group of
people but should be spread as widely as possible. One
of their favorite sayings was "Let knowledge be your

*An Arab classroom. Educa-
tion was valued highly by
the Muslim settlers in
Spain, and the achieve-
ments of their civilization
were many. Muslim
scholars made strides in the
fields of mathematics and
astronomy, and Muslim
physicians greatly advanced
the practice of medicine.*

possession and education your ornament." Education usually began at the age of five, when a child would learn to read and write at home, concentrating on the Koran, the holy book of Islam. Those whose parents were well off might continue to study at home under various tutors; others could study at the mosque, which served as a center of learning as well as worship. As Anwar Chejne relates in his book *Muslim Spain*, "[At the mosque the student] would receive his training in the Qur'an [Koran], Prophetic Traditions, jurisprudence, grammar, lexicography, and other related subjects. This training could be received at all levels and under seasoned teachers who often were renowned authorities in this or that discipline." The teachers maintained their level of excellence by traveling far and wide to others centers of learning throughout al-Andalus and the Middle East. Their watchword was "Seek knowledge even if it were in China." The pursuit of wisdom was also aided by the magnificent libraries established by Muslim rulers, who often competed with one another to see who could amass the largest collection of books.

Muslim scholars, inspired by books from Greece and India, delved deeply into mathematics and astronomy (the study of stars and planets). They are credited with producing the oldest existing book on arithmetic and algebra, and many of the star names (Algedi, Altair, Deneb) and astronomical terms (azimuth, nadir, zenith) now in use are derived from the Arabic language. As in the case of Hasdai ben Shaprut, the physicians of al-Andalus developed the practice of medicine to a high art; in the major cities, both in the East and in Spain, clean, well-supplied hospitals were open to all citizens, whether rich or poor.

Perhaps even more than their intellectual achievements, the people of al-Andalus were renowned for their ability to design and create beautiful objects,

from the smallest to the largest. Muslim craftsmen excelled at making leather goods, tools, cutlery, jewelry, glassware, and textiles. The ultimate expression of their skill was the architecture they created. From the moment they established themselves in Spain, the Muslims began building mosques, palaces, and bathhouses. According to the research of Anwar Chejne, at the beginning of the 10th century Córdoba boasted "1,600 mosques; 900 public baths; 60,300 mansions for notables, viziers [high executive officers], secretaries, commanders of the army; 213,077 houses for the people; and 80,455 shops." Most of these structures are long gone, but those that have survived—such as the Great Mosque of Córdoba, the Alcázar and the Giralda in Seville, and the Alhambra in Granada—testify to the brilliance of the Muslim

The lasting Muslim influence in Spain is most evident today in many impressive architectural achievements. Among them is the Alcázar, a 12th-century palace in Seville: shown here is the Hall of the Ambassadors, one of the Alcázar's many ornate chambers.

architects. The Alhambra, a rambling palace built during the 14th century in the hills above the southern city of Granada, is one of the architectural wonders of the world. Restored and preserved by the Spanish government, the Alhambra's exquisite chambers, courtyards, mosaics, fountains, and gardens provide dazzling proof of the refinement of Islamic civilization.

In view of their passion for building, it seems clear that the Muslims expected to remain in Spain forever. However, the descendants of the Visigoths had different ideas, and by the 10th century the tide was beginning to turn.

BORN IN A
FORTUNATE HOUR

Rodrigo Díaz, the man who became known as El Cid, was born in the early 1040s—scholars generally agree on 1043 as a good guess—in the town of Vivar. Vivar, now known as Vivar del Cid, is situated in the province of Castilla la Vieja (Old Castile), about six miles from the city of Burgos. In the words of Ramón Menéndez Pidal, the region consists of "vast tablelands, which, for one part of the year, are scorched by the sun, and for the other, suffer all the ravages of continual frost: 'nine months of winter and three of hell,' as the popular saying goes." Despite its punishing climate, the region was a wealthy one during the 11th century, known for its excellent wines and its abundant crops of corn.

The people of Vivar and its surrounding province were clearly descendants of the northern tribes; as recently as 1929, Menéndez Pidal could still describe them as typically fair haired, with blue eyes and aquiline features, the physical type known in Spain by the term *rubio* ("blond," as opposed to *moreno*, which means "dark haired"). It is impossible to say with any certainty what the area looked like in the 1040s, but Menéndez Pidal clearly felt that he had seen for himself the surroundings of Rodrigo Díaz's early years: "The ruddy color of the houses is that of the earth on which they are built; and in the summer the houses, with their plots of ground, are barely distinguishable among the fields of dull golden corn all around. Only a few poplars, on the banks of the Ubierna [River] or by the way-side, enliven the landscape with refreshing splashes of green."

Rodrigo's father, Diego Laínez, was a knight in the service of the king of Castile. Scholars have concluded that Diego Laínez was not in the highest ranks of the nobility, because his name does not appear on royal charters or on lists of the Castilian king's inner circle. Rodrigo's mother, although her first name was never recorded in any document that survives, came from a more prominent family than did her husband. Her father, Rodrigo Álvarez, was the lord of many castles, and his brother Nuño was an important figure in the court of the king of León. In deference to the importance of the Álvarezes, young Rodrigo was named after his maternal grandfather. (His surname, Díaz, simply means "son of Diego.")

Beyond these bare facts, little is known of Rodrigo's family or childhood. Various legends were later invented about the youth of El Cid by the jongleurs of the Middle Ages, traveling minstrels who entertained the nobility with singing, dancing, juggling, and recitations about the deeds of great heroes. Some of these stories—such as young Rodrigo's defeat of five Moorish kings or his early marriage to a certain Jimena Gómez after he had killed her father in a duel—were picked up by later writers, but none of them has any historical weight. Young Rodrigo's family was simply not important enough to inspire anyone to keep a detailed record of his childhood.

Historians do know with certainty, from various sources, what the customary life of a knight's son was

A 12th-century mosaic depicting the life of a knight. At about the age of 12, Rodrigo likely became a squire, or knight's assistant, caring for his lord's weapons, armor, and horses, thus learning the essentials of chivalrous life.

like in the Middle Ages. At the age of 12, Rodrigo would have become a squire, or knight's assistant. The duties of the squire were to ride out with the knight when he went to battle or simply ventured forth to seek his fortune. It was the squire's job to take care of the knight's weapons and armor and most of all to care for the horses. As the horse was the only means of transportation, it was extremely important that the knight's mounts be well fed and shod and that during long journeys tired horses be exchanged for fresh ones along the road. In this way, the young squires learned the basics of the chivalrous life.

Following this tradition, young Rodrigo would have been one of his father's squires when Diego Laínez fought with the Castilians against the forces of the king of Navarre, capturing the castles of Ubierna and Urbel and the village of La Piedra. Though Diego did not belong to the highest rank of the nobility, his exploits clearly impressed his monarch, King Ferdinand I. When Diego died in 1058 (presumably of natural causes), Rodrigo, then 15, became the ward of Ferdinand's eldest son, Sancho.

It is reasonable to assume that Rodrigo's mother's family, the Álvarezes, would have been more than able to support Rodrigo until he reached manhood. Therefore, the king's decision to provide for his knight's young son was not prompted by a desire to help a family in need. It grew from the central idea that made medieval society unique as a social system—the principle of lordship and vassalage.

European society had undergone a drastic change since the fall of the Roman Empire. For all the vast territory held by Rome, the wealth of the Empire had really been based upon Rome's control of the Mediterranean and the establishment of trade routes between East and West. When Rome fell, control of the Mediterranean passed to the Arab peoples of the Middle East. After the rise of militant Islam, the Arabs denied Europeans access to the sea, thus disrupting the entire pattern of trade that had sustained the Western world. This process has been traced by the Belgian historian Henri Pirenne in his *Economic and Social History of Medieval Europe*. According to Pirenne, "In the course of the eighth century the interruption of commerce brought about the disappearance of the merchants, and urban life, which had been maintained by them, collapsed at the same time." As the economy of the European cities collapsed, agriculture became increasingly important: "All classes of the population . . . lived directly or indirectly on the products of the soil, whether they raised them by their labor, or confined themselves to collecting or consuming them. . . . All social existence was founded on property or on the possession of land."

The emergence of land as the sole source of wealth caused a major shift in the political sphere. In the ancient world, the cities, most notably Athens, Rome, and Alexandria, were the centers of trade and therefore the centers of power. Individuals rose and fell according to their ability to form economic and political alliances and take advantage of daily events. The ability of orators to sway crowds in Athens, the ferocious treachery of imperial Rome's bloody power struggles, have been well documented by ancient authors. Those who gained influence over political or financial institutions enjoyed the fruits of rulership. However, when Rome and Athens declined and land became the sole measure of wealth, the power game was simplified. Those who possessed land only needed to hang onto it in order to preserve their influence; outsiders with ambition could either try to take someone else's land or, more easily arranged, serve a great lord who needed armed men to protect what was his.

In the new society, then, each lord needed vassals. The word *vassal* derived from an old Celtic word meaning "servant," but the medieval relationship between lord and vassal grew far more complex than the straightforward subordination generally implied by that term. At the core of that relationship was a pledge of mutual loyalty. The knight who became the vassal of a great lord agreed, among other things, to fight his lord's enemies. The lord, in return, promised to provide the knight with food and shelter when he needed it, reward him with land of his own, and care for his family in case of his death. The successful knight could then obtain vassals of his own—other knights who joined his retinue or peasants who lived on his land, paying him dues while they enjoyed his protection. In this system of mutual dependence, pledges of loyalty were supremely important, and double-dealing was roundly condemned. A knight's word of honor had an almost sacred power. Medieval life was often marked by brutality and ignorance, but the personal bonds that sustained it often caused people in later centuries—when all social relations, it seemed, began to revolve around money—to look back on the Middle Ages with intense nostalgia.

The fundamental code of 11th-century Spain thus dictated that King Ferdinand treat the young son of his dead knight as well as he treated his own son. By making Rodrigo the ward of the young prince Sancho, who was only a few years older, Ferdinand thus insured that the royal protection would last beyond his own lifetime. Meanwhile, Rodrigo was afforded the same advantages and privileges enjoyed by Sancho. For example, both boys were most likely educated in the royal castle by the local bishop. Perhaps surprisingly for one who was destined to make his way in life by the strength of his arm, Rodrigo appears to have been a decent student. As Menéndez Pidal points out, the mature Rodrigo's legal knowledge is proven by his service as a judge in at least one major case, although the one surviving example of his handwriting shows that he never completely mastered the art of penmanship.

There is no doubt that Rodrigo made steady progress in his duties as a squire and his studies of the art of war. Most squires had to wait until they were 20 to be knighted, but Rodrigo received the boon of knighthood from King Ferdinand in 1060, at the age of 17.

As the Middle Ages progressed, the ceremony of knighthood took on a solemn religious aspect, with a clergyman blessing the knight's sword in church. In 11th-century Spain, it was essentially a military ritual in which the knight's lord presented him with his weapons, fastening the sword around the knight's waist with his own hands. Beginning in the 11th century, the knight's sponsor often ended the ceremony by striking him across the neck or cheek with the flat of the hand. This curious custom was known as dubbing, after an old Germanic word meaning "to strike." The term eventually came to stand for the entire process of creating a knight. The French historian Marc Bloch has described the meaning of the act in his book *Feudal Society*:

> The contact thus established between the hand of the one who struck the blow and the body of the one who received it transmitted a sort of impulse—in exactly the same way as the blow bestowed by the bishop on the clerk whom he

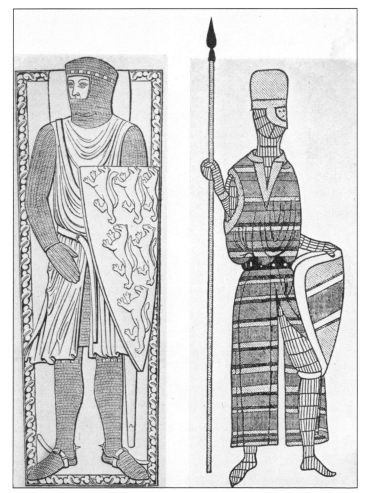

Medieval knights wearing suits of mail. The heavy, restricting plate armor worn by knights in battle after the 14th century developed from chain mail, made by joining hundreds of small metal rings. Although clearly less protective than plate armor, mail offered better ventilation and freedom of movement.

is ordaining priest. The ceremony often ended
with an athletic display. The new knight leapt on
his horse and proceeded to transfix or demolish
with a stroke of his lance a suit of armor attached
to a post; this was known as the *quintaine*.

The ceremony may well have had an added meaning
for young Rodrigo because he was now entitled to
wear his father's armor and carry his father's weapons.
The most important item of equipment, however, was
his horse. In the major Romance languages, the very
word for "knight"—*caballero* in Spanish, *chevalier* in
French, *cavaliere* in Italian—literally means "horse-
man." Without a horse, a man could not be a knight.
In this respect, Rodrigo may have found the king's
favor very useful. According to Menéndez Pidal, the
young knight's first warhorse cost 500 *mithqals*, a sum
that would have bought 50 oxen. Quite possibly the
horse came from the royal stables.

Throughout the *Poema de Mío Cid*, both the poet
and several characters employ the phrase *nacido en buen
ora* (born in a fortunate hour) to describe El Cid.
These words have the ring of a standard compliment,
the sort of tribute that was offered to anyone worthy
of deep respect. But in the case of El Cid or any other
great historical figure, it is literally correct. Everyone
who leaves a mark on history was essentially in the
right place at the right time. It was Rodrigo's fortune
to be born at a time when Spain needed a hero who
could become the symbol of its emerging national
identity.

Had Rodrigo been born in the town of Vivar two
or three centuries earlier, it is doubtful that anyone
would have remembered his name. Until the middle
of the 9th century, Castile itself had vitually no political importance. It was not a kingdom but rather
an undeveloped border area containing little more

than a handful of castles erected to repel occasional Muslim raids from the south. At that time, the kingdom of Asturias—roughly corresponding in area to the present-day provinces of Asturias and Galicia—was the focal point of Christian Spain. Asturias had gained this role in 718, when a Christian army under the Visigothic ruler Pelagius defeated the Muslims at the Battle of Cavadonga. After that, the Muslims confined themselves to the occasional raid and allowed Asturias to develop its political power and emerge as a center of Christian culture.

Castile grew to rival and finally surpass Asturias solely because of a power struggle within the Asturian realm. In 866, Alfonso III (also known as Alfonso the Great) ascended the throne of Asturias, only to be met with a revolt led by Froila, the count of Galicia. Expelled from his kingdom, Alfonso took refuge in the neighboring territory of Castile. Before long, Froila was murdered by Alfonso's supporters, and the deposed king was able to return. His exile had inspired him with the idea of expansion, and he soon began to settle his subjects in Castile, especially in the fertile valley of the Douro River. Under Alfonso, who reigned until 910, such former outposts as León, Toro, and Zamora became thriving fortified cities. Many of their inhabitants were Mozarabs from the south. The Mozarabs, already accustomed to living in the cities of al-Andalus, brought a new and undoubtedly exotic flavor to the northern territories.

To be sure, life in the new settlements was often rugged. The border regions were subject to continual attack by the Muslims, and the raids launched by the caliph Almanzor against León and Santiago at the end of the 10th century were especially devastating. In order to convince people to risk their lives and property in territories such as Castile, the Asturian rulers were forced to grant the settlers a good deal of autonomy, resulting in the development of rival political centers.

By continually sapping the strength of the Asturian kingdom, the Muslims played a significant role in the eventual development of Castile. Understanding the growing weakness of his neighbors, Sancho III Garcés of Pamplona, a small kingdom in the eastern part of Spain, seized the opportunity to expand his influence. He succeeded so well that by the time of his death in 1035 he was able to provide

A Muslim artifact from 10th-century Spain. At this time, the Muslims still controlled most of Spain— but the resistance to their rule, led by the Christian kings of Asturias, soon blossomed into the Reconquista.

a kingdom for each of his three sons, who became Ramiro I of Aragon, García III Sánches of Navarre (another name for Pamplona), and Ferdinand I of Castile, the man who knighted the young Rodrigo Díaz.

Outstripping his brothers in talent and ambition, Ferdinand quickly built Castile into Spain's most important kingdom. In 1037, only two years after claiming his inheritance, he absorbed the kingdoms of Asturias and León. At the same time, the Umayyad Empire in the south was splitting up into a number of smaller states, known in Arabic as *taifas*. Each of the major cities of al-Andalus—Córdoba, Toledo, Granada, Seville, and Valencia, among others—now became the capital of a separate taifa ruled by a Muslim king. Thus, the two rival political powers of the previous three centuries ceased to exist.

The simultaneous decline of Asturias and al-Andalus marked the beginning of a new era. As Roger Collins has expressed it, "Within a hundred years [from 1037] Spain was to be exposed to more new forces and influences than perhaps in the whole of its history since the coming of the Romans. . . . Like the fifth and eighth, and the sixteenth to follow, the eleventh century and early twelfth marked a period of profound change in the peninsula, in which the ideology of the *Reconquista* was first born."

In this period of upheaval, Rodrigo Díaz was to achieve legendary stature.

THE CAREER OF A KNIGHT

Rodrigo Díaz got his first chance to prove himself in battle in 1063, when he was 20 years old. The occasion arose from the rivalry between the kingdoms of Castile and Aragon. The Aragonese had captured the town of Graus, in the foothills of the Pyrenees Mountains, a territory under the control of al-Muqtadir, the Muslim king of Zaragoza. Al-Muqtadir appealed to Ferdinand, the king of Castile, for help. Clearly, the ideology of the Reconquista had not yet taken hold, because Ferdinand agreed to take up arms against his own brother, Ramiro of Aragon, on behalf of the Muslims.

Ferdinand's behavior was directed by two motives. First, he wanted to prevent his brother from using Graus as a base for further conquests; he knew that if Aragon expanded sufficiently, it would soon pose a threat to Castile. In other words, Ferdinand considered Zaragoza safer in the hands of the Muslims than in the control of his own brother. Second, Ferdinand expected to be paid handsomely for coming to the aid of al-Muqtadir. In the newly fragmented political world of 11th-century Spain, Christian rulers had discovered that there was much profit to be made

57

from the wealthy taifa states of al-Andalus. The Christians were not yet strong enough to think about recapturing the peninsula from the Muslims, but they were strong enough to launch destructive raids if they wanted to. The Muslim kings therefore adopted the tactic of paying Christian rulers regular sums of money, known as *parias*, in exchange for peace and quiet. The payment and acceptance of parias represented clever, hardheaded diplomacy on both sides, even if posterity has not regarded the practice with admiration.

It is not difficult to imagine Ferdinand upping his fee for attacking Graus, on the grounds that he was being asked to fight against his own flesh and blood. In any case, he got his price from al-Muqtadir and dispatched his eldest son, Sancho, to recapture Graus. Sancho, who stood to inherit both the Castilian throne and the parias from Zaragoza, had a considerable interest in curbing his uncle. Rodrigo Díaz was naturally included in the band of Castilian knights who ventured into the Pyrenees with the young prince. On May 8, 1063, the Castilians took the field against a group of Aragonese knights and defeated them soundly. King Ramiro himself was killed in the battle: according to one account, he was struck down by a spy who talked his way into the Aragonese camp and then thrust a lance into the king's eye. Ramiro would no longer be a problem for his relatives.

There is no record of Rodrigo's individual deeds at Graus, although it is safe to assume that he distinguished himself in battle and cemented his close relationship with Sancho. When Sancho succeeded to the throne after the death of Ferdinand in 1065, he immediately named Rodrigo the commander of his army. This post, known as *armiger* in Latin and *alferez* in Arabic, entitled Rodrigo to carry the royal sword in all processions. He also had a solemn duty, according to Menéndez Pidal, "to protect the rights of widows and orphans of noble birth and bring to justice any hidalgo [nobleman] who might transgress the law."

The latter duty was clearly more than symbolic, because Rodrigo was soon called upon to engage in single combat with Jimeno Garcés, a famous knight of Navarre. The combat was staged to settle a dispute between Castile and Navarre over a number of castles in one of the border regions. In the ancient world, such duels had been fought between picked champions to avoid a large-scale war or to settle a war that was causing both sides excessive casualties. The legendary combat between Hector and Achilles during the Trojan War, depicted in Homer's *Iliad*, is a classic example of this practice. When Achilles kills Hector, ties his body to the back of a chariot, and drags the slain warrior around the walls of Troy, the Trojans resign themselves to defeat.

In the Middle Ages, the duel took on a new dimension. It was seen not merely as a convenient way of settling disputes but also as a means of determining which party had justice on its side. For example, if one knight accused the other of a crime, hand-to-hand combat was the accepted way of settling the dispute. People believed that God, who knew the truth, would give strength to whichever man was in the right. To some, especially today, this logic may seem faulty, but Rodrigo certainly believed in it and profited by it. He defeated Garcés, boosting both his reputation and his wealth. As the victor in combat, he was entitled to hold Garcés prisoner until his friends or family paid a ransom for his release. Around the same time, Rodrigo killed a Muslim warrior from nearby Medinaceli. In this case, the rules of society entitled the victor to strip the unlucky Moor of everything on his back and all his possessions. Because bridles, saddles, and swords were often embossed with silver and gold, they had a value far above their everyday use.

As the king's armiger, Rodrigo also had the job of recruiting and training men for the king's service. Undoubtedly, Rodrigo's victories over Garcés and the Muslim knight made him both a persuasive recruiter and the sort of commander whose orders were quickly obeyed. King Sancho had steady employment for the men under Rodrigo's authority. According to the will of Ferdinand I, Sancho had received the kingdom of Castile; his brother Alfonso had inherited León; and the third brother, García, had taken possession of Galicia. Although Sancho was the eldest son, Alfonso had been his father's favorite. For this reason Ferdinand had given Alfonso León, the richest of the three regions. Following the family tradition, Sancho deeply resented this division of property. He had little love for either of his brothers and was determined to get León and Galicia for himself. García was his first victim. In 1071, Sancho formed an alliance with Alfonso, and the two brothers immediately invaded Galicia. They quickly deposed García, who took refuge in the Muslim kingdom of Seville.

Once García was out of the way, Sancho and Alfonso were ready for a head-to-head confrontation. They did battle at Golpejera in January 1072, and Sancho's forces carried the day. Sancho took Alfonso prisoner, then exiled him to Toledo, where he took up residence under the protection of the Muslim king. Sancho then proclaimed himself king of Castile, León, and Galicia, all the territory formerly possessed by his father.

These developments were highly advantageous for the king's armiger. As the 11th-century *Historia Roderici* states: "In every battle which King Sancho fought with King Alfonso . . . and defeated him,

Medieval knights invade a city. In 1072, El Cid fought bravely in the siege of Zamora, but his heroics did not save the life of his king, Sancho, who was murdered in his own camp.

Rodrigo bore the king's royal standard, and distinguished himself among the soldiers, and bettered himself thereby."

In other words, as Sancho grew wealthier and more powerful, so did Rodrigo. However, the king's family problems were not over, and his prosperity was to be short-lived. In the fall of 1072, Sancho's sister Urraca, no doubt acting under Alfonso's instructions, led a revolt against Sancho from the city of Zamora. Historians disagree as to whether Alfonso was actually in Zamora at this time, but he was almost certainly directing the rebellion. Sancho responded by marching on Zamora.

Because Zamora was protected on one side by the Douro River and encircled by thick stone walls, a direct attack was not prudent. Instead, Sancho followed the usual practice of medieval warfare and placed the city under siege. Medieval cities produced very little of their own food supply, depending instead on the surrounding countryside. By occupying the outlying areas and guarding the roads leading to the city, a besieging army could slowly starve the city's defenders into submission—a grim but highly effective procedure.

At Zamora, Rodrigo accomplished perhaps his greatest feat of arms. In the course of a siege, defenders would often ride out and try to catch the besiegers with their guard down. On one occasion, a group of 15 Zamoran knights set an ambush for Rodrigo, no doubt believing that they could greatly help their cause by killing Sancho's armiger. When the knights fell upon him, Rodrigo went back at them with lance and sword. After he killed one knight and hurled two more to the ground, the remainder spurred their horses and fled for their lives.

However, even Rodrigo's heroism could not save King Sancho from the fate that awaited him at Zamora. On October 7, a knight named Vellido Adolfo snuck into Sancho's camp and killed him with a lance. This treacherous act was an eerie repetition of the death that had met Ramiro I of Aragon nine years before, when as a young prince Sancho had besieged the town of Graus.

Alfonso quickly stepped into the vacuum created by his brother's death, returning from Toledo to assume the title Alfonso VI of León-Castile. Having just proved that exile was no guarantee of security, Alfonso decided to make sure that his surviving brother, García, would pose no future threat. In 1073 Alfonso summoned García to the Castle of Luna in

León and put him in chains, where the unfortunate man languished for 17 years, until his death in 1090.

The king's ferocity did not extend to his brother's armiger. According to the medieval code, a vassal could never be blamed for faithfully serving his lord. Indeed, the feats of arms Rodrigo had performed against Alfonso's men made him all the more valuable to the new regime. Alfonso therefore wasted no time in securing Rodrigo's services.

According to a tradition accepted by Menéndez Pidal, Rodrigo was not so eagerly swayed. He and the rest of Sancho's vassals were convinced that Alfon-

Upon the death of Sancho, his brother Alfonso became king and sought to·secure the services of El Cid. Legend has it that the knight, strongly suspecting Alfonso's hand in Sancho's murder, was not eager to join his entourage, but ultimately El Cid swore his allegiance to the new king.

so had engineered the treacherous murder of their king. Before he would give his allegiance to Alfonso, Rodrigo insisted that the king swear an oath, in the Church of Saint Gadea in Burgos, that he had not murdered his brother. After Alfonso repeated the oath three times, Rodrigo replied, "Then, if you swear falsely, may it please God that a vassal slay you even as the traitor Vellido Adolfo slew King Sancho."

Considering that Sancho had been not only Rodrigo's lord and patron but also his boyhood friend, the story is very appealing. However, it does have the flavor of fiction rather than fact, and modern historians such as Richard Fletcher are inclined to dismiss it out of hand. It is far more likely that although Rodrigo strongly suspected Alfonso's hand in the murder, he knew that there was no longer anything he could do for Sancho. Certainly he was aware that Sancho could no longer do anything for him; his only sensible move was to make peace with Alfonso and hope he would be treated with favor.

In the words of the *Historia Roderici*, "King Alfonso received [Rodrigo] with honor as his vassal and kept him in his entourage with very respectful attention." However, being treated with "very respectful attention" is not quite the same as being the king's right-hand man. Much as Alfonso may have valued Rodrigo, the king was also beholden to his vassals from León and to those who had helped him return to power, notably Pedro Ansúrez and García Ordóñez. A shrewd and cautious character, he was also aware that his original vassals had already proved their loyalty, whereas Sancho's men were only bowing to necessity. When Alfonso filled the post of armiger in 1072, his choice was not Rodrigo but a Leonese knight named Gonzalo Díaz.

Nevertheless, the king was mindful of his duty toward Rodrigo. He considered it his obligation to find a suitable wife for the knight and set about doing so. In either 1074 or 1075, Rodrigo was married to Doña (Lady) Jimena, a daughter of Duke Diego of Oviedo. Thus the king had allied Rodrigo with a family well up in the social scale: Doña Jimena was the great-granddaughter of Alfonso V of León and the niece of Alfonso VI.

If he was now allied to a family more illustrious than his own, Rodrigo also brought something to the match besides his fame as a knight. In the marriage settlement, which still exists in the archives of the cathedral in Burgos, Doña Jimena received half of her husband's property: her portion came to 3 entire towns in Castile and 34 properties scattered throughout the kingdom. When the couple's first child, Diego, was born, the king granted Rodrigo and all his descendants an exemption from royal taxes on the family land in Vivar and some other locations.

Records of Rodrigo's activities during the early part of Alfonso's 44-year reign are sketchy. Considering his military prowess, he may well have taken part in Alfonso's invasion of Navarre in 1076, an action that gained valuable territory for the Castilian monarchy. Surviving documents indicate that he was named to take part in two important legal cases during the 1070s, first as a judge and then as an advocate. These functions were reserved for prominent members of the royal court. The choice of Rodrigo also shows that his peers respected him for his knowledge and judgment as well as his valor in battle.

On the whole, it would appear that Rodrigo had much to be pleased about as he approached the age of 40. However, he clearly saw himself as deserving the kind of power and wealth usually reserved for kings. This he obtained before the end of his life, but in the short run his vaulting ambition nearly destroyed him.

Alfonso VI receives the advice of some of his counselors, many of whom warned the king against trusting El Cid, whose loyalty they believed still belonged to the slain Sancho. Fearing that he could not control the knight's ambition, the king banished El Cid in 1081.

EXILE

He will never love you, because he was your brother's courtier; he will always consider and prepare evil against you."

According to the *Carmen Campidoctoris*, a Latin document written during Rodrigo's lifetime, these words were often whispered in the ear of Alfonso VI by Rodrigo's rivals. Fortunately for Rodrigo, Alfonso had a mind of his own. Although the king never went so far as to put Rodrigo in charge of the royal army, he certainly treated the renowned knight as an honored vassal. These attentions were inevitably galling to courtiers such as García Ordóñez, whose ancestors had been great lords. These men considered Rodrigo a nobody who had gained rank, property, and a high-born wife solely because of his military skills. In their view, such a man could have no true principles or loyalty; he would serve any master who was willing to reward him.

There is no evidence that Rodrigo tried to develop allies at the court or undermine his critics. Typically, military heroes scorn the intrigues of politics and prefer the company of their fellow soldiers. Moreover, modesty is not always among their greatest virtues. Rodrigo was undoubtedly convinced that the men who outranked him in the king's service could never hope to defeat him in combat or equal his skill as a military commander. It is easy to imagine him pointing this out to them whenever he had the chance.

After he had enjoyed the king's favor for seven years, Rodrigo's pride and combativeness finally got him into trouble. In 1079, the king sent Rodrigo to collect the parias from al-Mutamid, the ruler of Seville. At the same time, a group of Castilian nobles journeyed to the kingdom of Granada, for a reason unknown to historians. They may have been acting on behalf of Alfonso, or they may have had some purpose of their own. When the nobles, each with a retinue of knights, arrived in Granada, they made up a sizable force. Granada's king, 'Abd Allah, persuaded the Castilians—undoubtedly with a promise of loot—to join him in a campaign against his enemy al-Mutamid. As the invaders began to pillage al-Mutamid's territory, Rodrigo sent 'Abd Allah a letter in Alfonso's name, asking him to withdraw. When this request was ignored, Rodrigo and his own knights took the field against the Granadans and defeated them outside the town of Cabra.

Rodrigo's actions in this affair were certainly in accordance with Alfonso's wishes: the king could hardly expect the Sevillians to pay him tribute money if he allowed his own knights to invade their territory. However, it appears that Rodrigo, undoubtedly thrilled to be back in action, may have savored his victory a bit too much for his own good. During the battle, he captured three of the Castilian nobles, along with a number of their knights. Among the nobles was García Ordóñez, one of Rodrigo's chief rivals.

Had Rodrigo been as much a politician as a warrior, he might have used his position of strength to make an ally of García. Instead, he seized his chance to enjoy a complete triumph over a man he con-

sidered his inferior in everything but social standing.
In the words of the *Historia Roderici*, "After his victory,
Rodrigo Díaz kept [the Castilian nobles] captive for
three days: then he deprived them of their baggage
and all their weaponry and set them free to go their
way." There could hardly have been any greater hu-
miliation for a man of García's status than to arrive
home with little more than the clothes on his back,
especially if the news of his defeat had preceded him.

When Rodrigo returned in triumph to Castile, he
found García and the other nobles he had humbled
working furiously against him. Evidently, Alfonso now
began to listen to Rodrigo's detractors. Perhaps he had
begun to perceive that Rodrigo, apparently invincible
on the battlefield, was not a man whose ambition
could be easily controlled. If such a formidable character should prove disloyal, the results could be dis-
astrous for Alfonso. Whether intentionally or not,
Rodrigo responded by stretching the king's tolerance
to the breaking point.

In 1081, a raiding party from the Muslim kingdom of Toledo crossed into Castile and sacked a castle
on the banks of the Douro. There was little chance
that the raid had been authorized by al-Qadir, the
Toledan ruler, because al-Qadir was virtually taking
orders from Alfonso at this point. Nevertheless,
Rodrigo hastily gathered a large band of knights—at
this point he commanded his own private army—and
invaded al-Qadir's territory, taking a large number of
captives and carrying off their possessions.

Even if Alfonso had been previously inclined to
give Rodrigo the benefit of the doubt, there was
no way he could ignore the invasion of Toledo. As
Richard Fletcher explains the situation:

> [Rodrigo's action] threatened the fragile equi-
> librium of the Christian king's protectorate [in
> Toledo]. It set a dangerous example to other

frontier lords among Alfonso's subjects. It invited counter-reprisals against the vulnerable garrisons of the fortresses recently acquired by Alfonso deep in Toledan territory. The king had to demonstrate his good faith towards al-Qadir and keep order on his marches [fortified borders]. It hardly needed the prompting of Rodrigo's enemies at court to persuade Alfonso that a public example must be made.

The king's solution was simple and severe. He banished Rodrigo from the kingdom.

Under the terms of his banishment, Rodrigo had nine days to remove himself from Alfonso's territory. It is not known what arrangements he made for Doña Jimena and his three children, Diego, Cristina, and María, but there was no necessity for them to leave with him. As Menéndez Pidal explains, banishment did not affect Rodrigo's possessions in Castile. He continued to be a subject of the king, enjoying the same rights of property. Alfonso's action had only broken the terms of Rodrigo's vassalage, the personal bond of protection and loyalty that existed between the knight and his king. Therefore, it is likely that

El Cid departs from the monastery of San Pedro de Cardeña, where he housed his wife and children during his exile. To make his way during this period, El Cid offered his services to the Christian rulers of Barcelona, who were eager to take control of the wealthy Muslim city-state of Zaragoza.

Rodrigo made some arrangement for the maintenance of family; according to the *Poema de Mío Cid*, he settled them in the monastery of San Pedro de Cardeña, not far from his birthplace of Vivar. Presumably this monastery had received generous endowments from Rodrigo; within its grounds, Doña Jimena and the children could live comfortably under the protection of the abbot. Rodrigo's real problem was providing for his own vassals.

Rodrigo's knights made up his *mesnada*, or retinue. Menéndez Pidal describes this group in the following terms: "The *mesnada* was composed, firstly, of those whom the lord brought up and whom, after knighting, he married and established; their duties of fealty were more stringent than those of the other vassals.... Next came the kinsfolk, who, since Germanic times, had for the most part represented the fighting strength of the company. . . . The lord of the *mesnada* also enrolled in his service friends and other such knights as might kiss his hand in token of their desire for his protection and pay."

The author of the *Poema de Mío Cid* writes that Rodrigo, once he had taken care of his family, held a banquet in San Pedro for his followers. As the news of his banishment spread throughout Castile, more than 100 knights mounted their chargers and galloped to join him. Elated at this show of support, Rodrigo rode out to welcome them. His words, as reproduced by the poet, were brief and to the point: "Hear me, my brave men, do not let what I say discourage you. I have only a small amount of money, but I shall share it with you. Bear this in mind like sensible men. Tomorrow at cock-crow have your horses saddled without delay. The worthy Abbot will ring for matins in San Pedro and will say the Mass of the Holy Trinity for us. When mass has been said we must prepare to ride away, for the days of grace are coming to an end and we have a good distance to cover."

Where were Rodrigo and his knights to go, and
how were they to survive? The second question was
the more easily answered: Because their only profes-
sion was that of warfare, they would survive by hiring
out their swords and capturing booty. The first question was somewhat difficult. Rodrigo, no doubt
hoping that Alfonso would rescind his banishment
before too long, was eager not to give the king any
further cause for complaint; therefore, he had to avoid
Seville, Granada, and Toledo. He decided that the
kingdom of Zaragoza, east of Castile, would provide
the best pickings, and he resolved to offer his services
to the Christian rulers of Barcelona, who were eager
to tap Zaragoza's riches.

Just before he left Castile, Rodrigo made a stop in
Burgos. There, according to the *Poema* at least, he
found an ingenious way to increase his supply of ready
money. Filling two handsome leather trunks with
sand, he convinced a pair of moneylenders that the
trunks were filled with gold. They were too heavy to
carry around, he said, and he wished to pawn them.
Knowing that Rodrigo had captured much treasure
from the Muslims, the moneylenders readily agreed to
give him 600 marks and promised not to open the
trunks for a year. They were so pleased with the deal

*A 19th-century painting
depicting a Moorish court-
yard. When the Christian
rulers of Barcelona turned
down the offer made by El
Cid, he approached the
Muslims, hoping they
would pay him for protec-
tion against the Christians.*

they had made that they even gave Martín Antolínez, one of Rodrigo's knights, a gift of 30 marks for acting as go-between. The story may or may not be true, but it neatly illustrates the early medieval condemnation of usury, the practice of lending money at interest. This attitude was to change after the 13th century, when trade revived and money became an important commodity again. In the time of El Cid, moneylenders were looked on as sinister characters, and a knight was entitled to cheat or rob them without any loss of honor.

Rodrigo's hopes of further profit in Barcelona were soon disappointed. Berenguer, the count of Barcelona, showed little interest in the exiled warrior or his offer of service. Always flexible, Rodrigo turned his attention to Zaragoza: if the Christians would not employ him to attack the Muslims, perhaps the Muslims would pay him for protection against the Christians.

Zaragoza, known as the White City because of the way its rising tiers of whitewashed houses shone in the moonlight, proved to be a fortunate choice. Al-Muqtadir, the longtime king of Zaragoza, had just died, leaving his kingdom to his two sons, al-Mu'tamin and al-Hayib. Al-Mu'tamin had inherited the better part of the kingdom, including the capital city; following the usual pattern, al-Hayib was determined to unseat his brother and take the whole kingdom for himself. When al-Hayib formed an alliance with the king of Aragon and the count of Barcelona, al-Mu'tamin knew that he needed help. He hired Rodrigo to organize the defense of his vulnerable borders in the east and the north.

During the summer of 1082, Rodrigo and his men twice defeated invading Aragonese forces, at Tamarite de Litera and Monzón. However, while he was engaged in these campaigns, al-Hayib and the

count of Barcelona were able to besiege the nearby
city of Almenar with a large army. Rodrigo undoubtedly relished the chance to show the count of Barcelona what sort of man he had turned down, but he
was first and foremost a practical military man. Feeling
that the invaders were too strong for his band of
knights, he advised al-Mu'tamin to buy them off.
Al-Mu'tamin agreed, but his brother, believing that a
military victory was in the offing, rejected the offer.
There was no choice but to fight.

The *Carmen Campidoctoris*, written not long after
these events, describes Rodrigo's battle gear as including a sword worked in gold, a lance made of ash
with a strong iron tip, a gold-embossed shield bearing
the image of a frightful dragon, and a helmet richly
decorated with gold and silver. The document does
not describe Rodrigo's strategy. However, the *Poema
de Mío Cid* tells of a second battle with Count Berenguer in a pine wood near Tévar, farther to the south.
Whether or not the poet's account of Rodrigo's
words to his men is historically accurate, it clearly
depicts the ingenuity of a clever commander in the
face of unfavorable odds:

> Tighten your saddle-girths and put on your
> armor. The enemy are coming downhill, all
> wearing hose (without boots). They have racing
> saddles and loose girths, but we shall ride with
> Galician saddles and wear boots over our hose.
> Though we number only one hundred knights
> we have got to defeat this large army. Before they
> reach the plain we shall attack with our lances.
> For each man you strike, three saddles will go
> empty.

Rodrigo's choice of equipment would have made it
much easier for his knights to keep their mounts than
would the enemy with their loose saddles and casual
footwear. The force of the Castilians' lance-blows
would have created a shock wave strong enough to

unhorse not only the man struck but also those behind him.

In the fighting at Almenar, Rodrigo's men captured the entire baggage train of the opposing forces—a rich haul in equipment, horses, and valuables—as well as Count Berenguer and his entire retinue of knights. As Richard Fletcher points out, Rodrigo had no authority to hold the count, much as he might have enjoyed doing so. He was obliged to turn Berenguer and his men over to al-Mu'tamin, who then negotiated a rich ransom for their release. Rodrigo himself would have received a healthy por-

A series of panels depicting Moors in battle. With the backing of the Muslim king of Zaragoza, al-Mu'tamin, El Cid won victory after victory against both Muslim and Christian forces, increasing the king's income and furthering his own reputation.

Four leaders of the First Crusade. Launched at the end of the 11th century, the First Crusade was a full-scale expedition to retake the city of Jerusalem from the Muslims and to spread Christianity to the unconverted.

tion of the ransom payment, enabling him to maintain his knights in style.

Following his remarkable victory at Almenar, Rodrigo took the offensive. With the backing of al-Mu'tamin, he raided both Aragon and the territory of al-Hayib. Between 1083 and 1085, he ravaged the lands of al-Mu'tamin's enemies, increasing his income and his reputation at the same time. When al-Mu'tamin died in 1085 and his son Ahmad al-Musta'in took the throne, Rodrigo's honored position at the court of Zaragoza remained unchanged. The young king certainly knew the worth of his Castilian ally, and he treated Rodrigo with undiminished respect.

If Rodrigo had any qualms about serving the Muslims at the expense of Christian rulers, no record of his misgivings has been preserved. As a man who had acquired a certain amount of learning along with his military skills, he was certainly aware that Muslim civilization was a good deal more refined than the society he had grown up in. The Zaragozan king al-Muqtadir, who had died just before Rodrigo's arrival, had been renowned as a poet, philosopher, mathematician, and astrologer. He had also built two magnificent palaces; the remains of one, the Aljafería, still stand in Zaragoza. Alfonso VI, like Rodrigo the product of a rough frontier culture, could hardly measure up to these standards.

Rodrigo was unquestionably aware of the conflict between his own religion, Roman Catholicism, and Islam. In 1064, when Rodrigo was a young knight, Pope Alexander II had dispatched an international force to capture the Muslim stronghold of Barbastro, a city in the Pyrenees Mountains. The Christian knights, mostly French and Italian, captured the city and slaughtered most of its Muslim inhabitants. The conquerors then proceeded to live in luxury, scandalizing the Christian clergy by organizing the surviving Muslim women into harems. The following year, al-Muqtadir of Zaragoza recaptured the city and in turn slaughtered its entire garrison. A young knight hearing of these events might well have concluded that there was not always a vast moral difference between Christians and Muslims.

Jerusalem, depicted here in a medieval manuscript, is a place of both literal and symbolic importance for Christians. That the sacred city was in the hands of Muslims at the end of the 11th century was an outrage for Christian zealots of the period.

Even though Christians and Muslims enjoyed many years of coexistence in Spain, the thought of reconquest grew rapidly—both in Spain and in the rest of Europe—during the 11th century. (Ironically, this idea had grown from the Muslim concept of *jihad*, or holy war, which had inspired Muhammad to conquer the Middle East and North Africa.) By the end of the century (in 1093), the Roman church had launched the First Crusade, a full-scale expedition whose aim was to retake the sacred city of Jerusalem, the scene of Jesus' crucifixion and resurrection, from the Muslims. In Spain, the crusading urge found its philosophical focus in the cult of Santiago, or Saint James the Great.

Saint James the Great was one of the 12 Apostles, the followers of Jesus who went forth from Jerusalem to spread the teachings of Christianity. According to legend, when Saint James died, his corpse was placed in a stone coffin by his followers and set afloat on the sea. The coffin eventually washed up on the shores of northwestern Spain, where Saint James had once preached, and was buried by local Christians. The grave was forgotten soon afterward and was not re-discovered until 813, when a Christian bishop was guided to its location by a bright star. On this site grew the cathedral city of Santiago de Compostela (*compostela* means "field of the star"), which became the focus of mass pilgrimages during the Middle Ages and still draws worshipers from all over the world.

Saint James allegedly appeared to Christian troops during a battle in 844, inspiring them to defeat a force of Muslim raiders. After this, the saint took on a military as well as a religious aspect, becoming known as Santiago Matamoros, or Saint James the Moor Killer. After two centuries, Saint James replaced Saint Eulalia, an early Christian martyr, as Spain's patron saint. In 1170, Christian knights formed the Order of

A Christian bishop baptizes pagans. In Spain, the spirit of the Crusades was vested in the cult of Santiago, or Saint James the Great, one of the 12 Apostles of Jesus who spread the teachings of Christianity and whose coffin, according to legend, washed up on the shores of northwestern Spain.

Santiago and dedicated themselves to defending their land and religion against the Muslims.

By the mid-1080s, Alfonso VI of León-Castile, Spain's most powerful Christian monarch, opened a vigorous assault on al-Andalus. After a bitter yearlong siege, he captured the city of Toledo, which had been in the hands of the Muslims for 370 years. Emboldened by his success, Alfonso launched further expeditions into other Muslim territories. In 1086, he personally led his army up to the walls of Zaragoza and besieged the city. By doing so, the king set the stage for a direct confrontation with his former vassal, Rodrigo. Rodrigo, never one to surrender, would undoubtedly have ventured forth at some point to do battle with his former master. This clash of strong-willed men would have provided the poets and chroniclers with rich material, but it never took place. An unexpected crisis brought Rodrigo and his monarch together again.

CHAPTER
SIX

LORD OF VALENCIA

El Cid watches as his men carry out an execution on his orders. In 1095, after torturing and questioning the former ruler of Valencia, Ibn Jahhaf, about a missing hoard of treasure, the ruthless El Cid buried him in the ground up to his armpits and then had him roasted alive.

The crisis that impelled King Alfonso to repair his relations with El Cid arose like a whirlwind out of Africa, in the form of the Almoravids. As recently as 1040, no one had ever heard of these people, for the best of reasons: they did not exist. Even today, historians have little to go on when discussing the history of the Almoravids, whose civilization vanished after little more than a century, leaving few records behind.

According to Richard Fletcher's researches, the Almoravids owed their existence to a Muslim holy man named Ibn Yasin. Around 1039, Ibn Yasin journeyed from Arabia into the vast Sahara Desert in northwestern Africa, at the bidding of a tribal leader who wished his people to receive religious instruction. Ibn Yasin was a fundamentalist: he preached strict obedience to the law of Islam, which permitted very little in the way of physical comfort or enjoyment. The rough nomadic tribespeople of the Sahara cared very little for this message; when Ibn Yasin's sponsor died, they burned the teacher's house and drove him away. Ibn Yasin then found his way to the Atlantic coast of Africa and founded a religious community known as a *ribat*. There he had great success in making converts, and his numerous followers soon became known in Arabic as al-Murabitun (the people of the ribat), a name that speakers of medieval Spanish transformed into Almoravid.

As he gathered strength, Ibn Yasin returned to the scene of his previous defeats and conquered the Saharan tribes, converting them forcibly to his version of Islam. After Ibn Yasin's death in battle in 1059, Yusuf ibn Tashufin took command of the Almoravids in the northern desert. By 1079, Yusuf had pushed across the Atlas Mountains and had made himself the master of North Africa. He was now peering at Spain across the Straits of Gibraltar.

Yusuf, the rough-hewn desert warrior, was a far cry from the refined, intellectual Muslim kings of al-Andalus. Drawing on Arabic sources, Menéndez Pidal describes the Yusuf of 1079 as "an old man of seventy, lean and swarthy, with brows that met, a straggling beard, and a piping voice. . . . His only fare was barley bread, milk, and camel's flesh; his only clothing was of wool, and he wore a veil over his face after the manner of the desert tribes."

Yusuf's crude appearance and his ignorance of literature, science, and the arts made him an object of ridicule throughout the Muslim world. Nevertheless, the rulers of al-Andalus turned to him as a savior. They understood that the refinements of their culture had sapped the warlike zeal that had gained them their empire in Spain. Now their enemy Alfonso had taken Toledo and was threatening Seville and Zaragoza, and no one but Yusuf had the strength to stop him. As al-Mu'tamid, the ruler of Seville, declared when warned that Yusuf was as likely to oust him from his throne as was Alfonso: "I would prefer anything rather than be accused of surrendering Al Andalus to the Christians, to have it turned into a colony of infidels [un-believers]; I do not want to be cursed from the pulpit of every mosque of Islam; and, since I am bound to choose, I would sooner be a cameleer with the Almoravids than a swineherd amongst the Christians."

A mosaic depicts a Christian and a Muslim in battle. When the Muslim leader Yusuf ibn Tashufin landed on the southern coast of Spain in June 1086, King Alfonso moved to meet the Muslim threat. Their armies clashed outside the city of Badajoz in October 1086.

Accepting the invitation of his Muslim cohorts, Yusuf landed on the southern coast of Spain in late June 1086. When Alfonso learned that Yusuf was advancing on Seville, he quickly lifted his siege on Zaragoza and gathered an army. He did not, however, try to heal his rift with Rodrigo at this time, believing that he had sufficient strength to beat back any Muslim threat. Marching southward, Alfonso encountered the Muslims near Sagrajas, about five miles from the city of Badajoz, and attacked them on October 23.

Yusuf sent the troops of his Muslim allies into battle first, but they were no match for the Christians, who slaughtered them right and left. Yusuf made no attempt to intervene; he despised the Muslims of al-Andalus as much as he despised the Christians. He held his own troops back until he saw that Alfonso's men, carried away by their success, were a long distance from their camp. Then he swept in behind them, sacked the camp, and began a rout that ended with Alfonso and 500 of his knights, all wounded, withdrawing from the field of battle in the dark of night.

The ferocity and discipline of the Almoravid troops, combined with their nerve-wracking yells and drumbeats, had proved too much for Alfonso's supposedly invincible army. According to Menéndez

Pidal, Yusuf had his men decapitate all the Christians slain on the field of Sagrajas and gathered the severed heads into mounds, from which the muezzins called the Almoravid troops to their morning prayers. Alfonso finally understood the strength and determination of his enemy, but it appeared to be too late. Toledo, Seville, and the rest of al-Andalus lay open to the Almoravids.

To the amazement of all, Yusuf suddenly decided to return to Africa instead of following up his victory. The presumed reason for this decision was the death of his only son, who had remained behind in North Africa because of illness. Nevertheless, the Battle of Sagrajas had changed the balance of power on the peninsula. Yusuf left 3,000 Almoravid knights in Spain under the command of al-Mu'tamid of Seville, who along with the other Muslim rulers immediately ceased all payment of parias to Alfonso.

Humbled in battle and deprived of considerable income, Alfonso was now a desperate man. He made an appeal to France in the form of a veiled threat, stating that unless he received help he would have to make peace with the Muslims and allow them to invade French territory. The French promised troops, but their aid was slow in coming. Alfonso then turned to his former vassal Rodrigo, who was still serving the Muslims in Zaragoza. The king and his exiled knight met in Toledo at the end of 1086. Although Rodrigo reportedly kneeled in submission before the king, he had the upper hand and made the most of it. The agreement between the two men placed several castles in the hands of Rodrigo and further decreed that any land he took from the Moors would belong to him and all his descendants. These terms were exceptionally generous, and they represented a great triumph for a man who had been sent packing five years earlier.

The reconciliation lasted two years, during which there is almost no record of Rodrigo's doings. By 1089, the Muslims of al-Andalus, whose fear of Rodrigo had caused them to resume their tribute payments to Alfonso, had persuaded the dreaded Yusuf to return to Spain. Joining with existing Muslim forces, Yusuf and his Almoravids besieged the Christian outpost of Aledo, in southeastern Spain. Alfonso, his troops now reinforced by French knights, set out to relieve Aledo and ordered Rodrigo to join him there with his own men. Somehow, the Christian forces failed to connect. The mix-up had no military consequences, because Yusuf withdrew as soon as Alfonso's army arrived on the scene. However, Rodrigo's old enemies in the Castilian court—who must have been deeply annoyed by his ability to squeeze so many valuable concessions out of the king—persuaded Alfonso that Rodrigo had missed the rendezvous on purpose, in the hope that Alfonso's forces would be wiped out by the Almoravids.

Alfonso, perhaps regretting his forced generosity to Rodrigo, believed the accusers. Rodrigo drew up a number of legal documents asserting his innocence, requested a formal trial, and also offered to fight a judicial duel with any one of his accusers. Menéndez Pidal indicates that under 11th-century law, Rodrigo's sworn oath, as contained in the documents, should have been enough to exonerate him. However, Alfonso had no wish to be appeased. He ignored Rodrigo's petitions, ordered him out of Castile for the second time, confiscated all his properties, and even imprisoned his family for a short time.

During his first exile, Rodrigo had at least enjoyed the option of selling his services to the Muslims. He now found that avenue closed. He had offended al-Mu'tamin, his former patron at Zaragoza, by going back to Alfonso, and the Muslim ruler expressed no interest in rehiring him. Rodrigo's only choice was to head for the southeast coast, known as Levante.

Powerful forces stood in his way. al-Mu'tamin, knowing well how dangerous Rodrigo could be, formed an alliance with Count Berenguer of Barcelona, his former enemy. Berenguer, still smarting over his defeat by Rodrigo seven years earlier, needed little urging to take the offensive. His powerful army attacked Rodrigo's forces at Tévar in 1089, but Rodrigo remained invincible. Once again, he took Berenguer prisoner, capturing as well the count's magnificent sword, Colada, said to be worth a small fortune in itself. Rodrigo used the sword for the rest of his life, making its name legendary throughout Spain.

The *Poema de Mío Cid* paints an amusing picture of Rodrigo as a captor, claiming that his only condition for releasing the count was that Berenguer sit down to a banquet with him. Considering the scorn with which the haughty count had treated Rodrigo in the past, the story may not be so far-fetched: partaking of Rodrigo's food under these circumstances was certainly a symbol of submission. According to the poet, Berenguer resisted for three days, refusing to touch a morsel; when he finally gave in, Rodrigo sat and watched him, insisting that he down his food with gusto. "I have not eaten so heartily since I became a count," Berenguer declared after the meal, "and I shall never forget how good it tasted."

There was, of course, one more condition for Berenguer's release—the payment of a huge ransom. As the count rode off, vowing never to cross swords with Rodrigo again, the victorious knight understood the advantage of operating on his own: this time, all the ransom money went into his own coffers.

With Berenguer eliminated as a counterforce, nothing stood between Rodrigo and the rich territories of Levante. Almost to a man, the Muslim rulers of the region hastened to place their territories under Rodrigo's protection and to fill his pockets with tribute money. Rodrigo established his base of operations in the region between Morella and Teruel, occupying towns whose present-day names bear witness to his domination—Lucena del Cid, Iglesuela del Cid, El Poyo del Cid, Villafranca del Cid. His greatest prize was Valencia, the wealthy city on the shores of the Mediterranean, whose ruler, al-Qadir, had once been the puppet of King Alfonso. Now al-Qadir virtually placed Valencia in the hands of Rodrigo, paying 52,000 dinars a year for the privilege of being his servant.

Rodrigo had gained mastery over Levante, but Levante was now surrounded by hostile forces. In addition to Alfonso and al-Mu'tamid in the north, Rodrigo had to contend with the Almoravids to the south and west. Yusuf had been relatively quiet since his return to Spain, but he had pledged to recapture Toledo, and his support among the Muslim masses was growing. The religious leaders of Islam were drawn to the rock-ribbed faith professed by the Almoravids and increasingly expressed their disgust with the more liberal ways of the taifa kings. While under attack from the religious faction, the taifa kings were losing the support of their ordinary subjects, who found themselves paying colossal taxes so that the kings could maintain their opulent palaces and send tribute money to Rodrigo.

Beginning in 1089, the Almoravids began to gobble up territory in the south. Within three years, Yusuf had taken Granada, Málaga, Seville, and Córdoba and was encamped a mere 22 miles south of Valencia. The city was still under the control of Rodrigo's man al-Qadir, but in the fall of 1092 a pro-Almoravid party staged a successful coup. The rebels executed al-Qadir and proclaimed Ibn Jahhaf, a prominent judge, ruler of Valencia.

Rodrigo, who had been campaigning in Zaragoza, understood that Valencia was on the verge of passing into the hands of the Almoravids. He hurried back to the south and in July 1093, after securing the surrounding countryside, laid siege to Valencia. Ibn Jahhaf appealed to Yusuf for aid, but the Almoravid leader was occupied in the western half of the peninsula. By May 1094, conditions in Valencia had become intolerable, with people falling dead from starvation in the middle of the street. Ibn Jahhaf had no choice but to surrender the city to Rodrigo.

At first, Rodrigo proved to be a mild ruler, reducing taxation to the limits set by Islamic law and staffing his garrison with Mozarabs, who were more respectful of Muslim customs than other Christians. The populace were certainly grateful and relieved, first of all to have food on their tables and then to find that their new master was not a bloodthirsty avenger. However, Rodrigo could not have had too many illusions about where their sympathies lay as long as the Almoravids remained a power in Spain. According to the *Poema*, he wasted no time in declaring his continuing loyalty to Alfonso, claiming that he would not cut his long, flowing beard until the king had pardoned him. Rodrigo backed up this statement by dispatching Alvar Fáñez to Castile with a gift of 1,000 horses and a considerable sum of money. Alfonso's heart was softened to the extent of allowing Rodrigo's wife and children to join him in Valencia, where they witnessed his spectacular victory over Yusuf and the Almoravids at Cuarte in October 1094.

Once the Almoravids were eliminated as a military threat, Rodrigo turned his attention to securing the countryside and governing Valencia. Few records of his rule survive, but it appears to have taken a very harsh turn. After Cuarte, he no longer needed to cultivate the loyalty of the Valencian Muslims. Now that he had enjoyed his crowning achievement as a military man, he reverted to the second overwhelming concern of his adult life—enriching himself and his vassals. Even the admiring Menéndez Pidal acknowledges that Rodrigo was now possessed by a "lust for wealth."

According to Richard Fletcher, Rodrigo imprisoned the richest citizens of the city and released them only when they had paid him 200,000 gold mithqals. However burdensome this may have been, the men who bought their freedom fared much better than their former ruler Ibn Jahhaf. Rodrigo's displeasure with Ibn Jahhaf was twofold: First, Ibn Jahhaf had killed the former king, Rodrigo's client al-Qadir.

El Cid and his men enter the pine forest of Tévar, where they defeated the count of Barcelona. As governor of Valencia, El Cid concentrated on increasing his personal wealth as well as that of his vassals. One of his practices was to imprison the richest citizens of the city and demand large quantities of gold in exchange for their release.

Equally important, he had presumably taken possession of al-Qadir's fortune, which Rodrigo was determined to have. Ibn Jahhaf had turned over some of the
money when he surrendered the city, but Rodrigo
believed there was more to be had. In 1095, Rodrigo
had Ibn Jahhaf questioned under torture about al-
Qadir's treasure; then, having obtained the informa-
tion he wanted, he condemned the Muslim to death.
Even at that, an ordinary execution—a quick behead-
ing, for example—was not enough to satisfy Rodrigo.
He had Ibn Jahhaf buried in the ground up to his
armpits and then ordered his men to light a fire
around the condemned man, roasting him alive. Eye-
witnesses reported that Ibn Jahhaf reached out and
drew the burning brands closer to his body, hastening
his death. According to Fletcher, "Rodrigo was with
difficulty restrained from inflicting the same fate upon
his victim's wife and children."

No such fate befell Rodrigo's own family. Little is
known of Doña Jimena during this period, but it may
be assumed that she was happier as the uncrowned
queen of Valencia than as the wife of an exile. When
Rodrigo's daughters, Cristina and María, reached
marriageable age—quite an early age in those days—
their father made illustrious matches for them. His
choice for Cristina was Ramiro, a high-ranking noble
from Aragon: Cristina and Ramiro's son García eventually became king of Navarre, although Rodrigo was
long gone by that time. María married Ramón Berenguer III of Barcelona, thus cementing the peaceful
relations between the counts of Barcelona and the
lord of Valencia. Rodrigo's son, Diego, as the heir to
his father's now considerable fortune, was quite a
desirable match as well. All that is known, however, is
that Diego died in battle in 1097, while in the service
of King Alfonso. It may be assumed from this that
Rodrigo and his monarch were finally reconciled,

although there is no evidence that Rodrigo ever again considered himself Alfonso's vassal.

By all accounts, the lord of Valencia lived like a king in his own right, sitting in a chair of carved ivory that had belonged to the Muslim rulers of Toledo and receiving guests in halls richly hung with tapestries and precious textiles. Apparently, he never did trim his flowing beard and was no less imposing in his palace than he was on the battlefield. The *Poema de Mío Cid* describes his civilian outfit as including "a linen shirt, snow-white and fastened neatly at the wrist with gold and silver links. . . . Over this undergarment he wore an elegant silk gown beautifully worked in gold brocade. His fur-lined coat was red, with fringes of gold. . . . He covered everything with a cloak so rich that it would attract the attention of all beholders." Doña Jimena was no less magnificent, wearing an 8th-century jeweled girdle that had once belonged to Sultana Zobeida of Baghdad—this was one of the hidden treasures that had cost Ibn Jahhaf his life.

Despite the somewhat oriental splendor of his court, Rodrigo did his best to advance Christianity in Valencia. He made no attempt to interfere with the worship of Islam, but he did convert the Great Mosque of Valencia to a Christian church. He also used his influence to further the career of Bishop Jerónimo, the militant clergyman who before the Battle of Cuarte begged to strike the first blow at the Almoravids. Rodrigo was once quoted as vowing that "a Rodrigo [King Roderic of the Visigoths] lost this peninsula, and a Rodrigo shall regain it."

Whether he could have achieved this lofty ambition remains a matter of speculation. Rodrigo Díaz died peacefully in his bed in Valencia in 1099.

THE LEGEND OF EL CID

Early in the 20th century, Ramón Menéndez Pidal described the aftermath of the hero's death in the following terms:"In those days, when society was based upon ties of kindred and vassalage and all events were invested with the importance of Providence, the expression of grief assumed proportions that to us are inconceivable. The men beat their breasts, rent their garments, and tore out their hair; the women scratched their faces until the blood flowed, and covered their foreheads with ashes, and the weeping and wailing went on for many days."

Valencia's fate remained in the balance, and Doña Jimena emerged from her period of mourning determined to maintain the city as a Christian stronghold. Apparently, she enlisted the support of Alfonso VI in this undertaking. By 1102, however, the Almoravids were once again at the walls of the city, under the command of a general named Mazdali. Without Rodrigo to lead the Christian forces, there was little chance of resisting the Muslim onslaught. Alfonso decided that there was no choice but to abandon Valencia. (The city remained in Muslim hands until 1238, when it was retaken by King Jaime I of Aragon.)

Richard Fletcher has imaginatively reconstructed the scene of departure:

> The long caravan of carts and litters, camels, horses, mules and donkeys, jolted off over the level lands of the *huerta* [cultivated fields] with its escort of troops. The king had detailed some of his soldiers to stay behind and fire the city. As Mazdali's men watched from the higher ground to the south they would have seen the wreaths of smoke arise, soon to billow into thick black clouds. By the time they re-entered the charred remains of Valencia, Rodrigo's body would have been well on its way back home to Castile.

Doña Jimena had her husband's body reburied in the monastery at San Pedro de Cardeña and lived nearby until her own death, which probably occurred in 1116. This date marks the end of the factual history of Rodrigo Díaz and his family; there is no further record of his daughters.

It would be tempting to say that Rodrigo's exploits changed the history of Europe, or at least the history of Spain, but this would be stretching a point. As far as Europe was concerned, the conquest of Jerusalem by the Crusaders in 1099, only five days after Rodrigo's death, was far more significant; the reopening of the Mediterranean allowed a gradual revival of trade, leading to the flowering of medieval civilization in Europe during the 13th century. As for Spain itself, Rodrigo's victory at Cuarte certainly stemmed what appeared to be an irresistible advance by the Almoravids. But the military power of the Muslims in the peninsula was not decisively broken until 1212, when Alfonso VIII of Castile crushed a Muslim army at Las Navas de Tolosa. The final chapter of the Reconquista, the expulsion of the Muslims (as well as the Jews) by Ferdinand and Isabella, did not unfold until 1492, nearly four centuries after Cuarte.

Rodrigo's greatest legacy may be the growth and survival of his legend. It is difficult to think of another historical figure whose deeds and character have so consistently captured the imagination of later generations, both in his own country and abroad. (Britain's King Arthur has perhaps inspired more legends, but Arthur, like Achilles, is a semimythical figure whose actual existence is a subject of debate among scholars.) Aside from the *Carmen Campidoctoris* and the *Historia Roderici*, straightforward biographies written during his lifetime, the first literary mention of Rodrigo was made in a Latin poem dating from 1147. In this poem, Rodrigo is referred to for the first time in print as "my Cid." Apart from establishing the title that would eventually replace his given name, the brief poem adds little to the hero's luster.

Rodrigo owes his enduring fame to the *Poema de Mío Cid*, one of the masterpieces of medieval literature. Written sometime between 1175 and 1207, the *Poema* begins with El Cid's exile and ends with his triumphant return to Castile as lord of Valencia. Many historical events, details, and personages are included in the poem, and the author (whose identity is also a matter of debate) was intimately acquainted with

El Cid displays the head of his fiancée's father in an illustration based on a scene from the play Le Cid, *by the 17th-century French dramatist Pierre Corneille. For centuries after El Cid's death, artists and writers contributed to the elaborate legend surrounding his life.*

Castile and its geography. On balance, however, the *Poema de Mío Cid* cannot be taken too literally.

Nearly half the poem's 4,000 lines, for example, describe El Cid's conflict with the princes of Carreón, a pair of cowardly layabouts who marry and then brutalize his daughters; after much struggle, El Cid obtains a legal judgment against the princes and then marries his daughters to more illustrious husbands. This story makes exciting reading—rather too exciting to be believable, despite the efforts of Menéndez Pidal to prop it up with historical evidence. The family of Carreón was indeed prominent in 11th-century Castile, but present-day scholars forcefully reject the idea that any of them was ever married to a daughter of El Cid. In any case, if the princes had been foolish enough to insult Rodrigo as grossly as they do in the poem, it is hard to believe that the warlike Cid would have taken them to court: more likely, he would have tracked them down and killed them at the first opportunity, whatever the consequences.

The poet's concern was first of all to create an appealing work of art, and in this he succeeded brilliantly. The fast-paced narrative has all the timeless ingredients of best-sellerdom—heroic warriors, despicable villains, damsels in distress—and the quick, pulsing rhythms of the original Spanish text make the work as compelling today as it must have been for medieval audiences. Equally important, the poet was writing what might be called a tract for the times. The Castile of his day was wracked by civil conflict and under continued pressure from the Muslims, and the poet clearly intended the story of El Cid to instruct and inspire his fellow citizens.

In the *Poema*, El Cid is not only a great warrior. He is above all a man of honor, a devout Christian, and a loyal subject of his king. Describing El Cid's capture and release of Count Berenguer, for example, the poet writes: "The Count set spurs to his horse and rode off, turning his head to look back for fear the Cid should change his mind—a thing that famous man would not do for anything in the world, for never in his life had he gone back on his word." Nor would he ever turn his back on his king, no matter how unjustly he might be treated. El Cid keeps sending gifts to Alfonso throughout the poem, and even after conquering Valencia, there is nothing more he wants than to be restored to the king's good graces. When the two men finally meet, the following scene takes place:

> As soon as the Cid caught sight of the King he ordered all his men to halt, while he . . . dismounted, and then he carried out what he had planned to do. He knelt down on his hands and knees on the ground and with his teeth he pulled up a mouthful of grass. With tears of joy streaming from his eyes he showed in this way his complete submission to his liege lord.

El Cid's loyalty is completely rewarded in the end when the king undertakes to see justice done in the matter of his daughters. The princes of Carreón, who have little to recommend them but their noble blood, fall into disgrace. El Cid, the man of humbler birth who honors his king and fights the Muslims, emerges triumphant. There is no way of knowing whether these earnest lessons changed the attitude of the people of Castile. However, if the poet was still alive when the Castilians broke the power of the Moors at Las Navas de Tolosa, no one could have blamed him for believing that his artful propaganda had played a part in the victory.

As the tide of Christianity began to advance during the 13th century—bracketing the recapture of Valencia, the Castilians took Córdoba in 1236 and Seville in 1248—Spaniards even began to regard El

Cid as a saint. Not surprisingly, the cult of El Cid was created by the monks of Cardeña, who possessed his remains. (The coffins of Rodrigo and Jimena have since been removed to the cathedral at Burgos, to which El Cid supposedly once made a gift of a boot filled with silver.) The monastery continues to exhibit various relics of El Cid to the present day, although the monks' campaign to have him canonized by the Catholic church fizzled out during the 16th century.

Although El Cid apparently never seriously threatened to replace Saint James as the patron saint of Spain, his legend grew with the passing centuries. As the Reconquista was completed and Spain began to build its empire in the New World, no one could have been a better model for the swashbuckling conquerors of Peru and Mexico than the pious, patriotic, courageous El Cid. (Not to mention the real-life Rodrigo Díaz, with his passion for wealth and power.) As Richard Fletcher points out, the *Romancero del Cid*, a collection of the hundreds of ballads composed about El Cid during the Middle Ages, was reprinted 26 times after its publication in 1605. In an age when much of the population of Europe was unable to read and write, the popularity of this work is all the more striking.

El Cid enjoyed a triumph on the stage in 1636, when the French dramatist Pierre Corneille placed him at the center of his drama *Le Cid*. Drawing upon an earlier drama by the Spanish author Guillén de Castro—who had been inspired in turn by the Spanish ballads of the Middle Ages—Corneille portrayed El Cid as a man torn between the demands of his heart and the demands of honor. In *Le Cid*, Rodrigue, as he is called in French, is obliged to kill the father of his beloved, Chimène, in a duel caused by an insult to Rodrigue's family. Chimène is then obliged to reject Rodrigue out of loyalty to her own family. The two lovers agonize over the social ideals

El Cid died peacefully in 1099, but the courageous knight was immortalized some 100 years later, when an unknown Spaniard wrote the Poema de Mío Cid, *a poem that recounts several of his finest hours as a soldier, praising him as an exemplary vassal of noble character.*

that outweigh their personal feelings, until the king provides a happy ending by ordering Chimène to marry Rodrigue, who is about to serve his country by fighting the Muslims. *Le Cid* enjoyed tremendous success in the Paris of its day and quickly became one of the classics of world literature. Although it diverges widely from historical truth, it testifies to the staying power of El Cid's heroic image in an age when medieval ideals were fast disappearing.

Early in the 19th century, when many writers and artists looked back on the Middle Ages as a kind of lost paradise, El Cid shone as brightly as ever. Europe was approaching the age of the Industrial Revolution; concepts such as honor and loyalty were quickly declining in a society divided into employer and employee, debtor and creditor. In addition, a number of modern nations were beginning to emerge, and their citizens were in need of national heroes. The Swiss historian Johan Müller, for example, wrote of El Cid in 1805: "All that godliness, honor, and love could make of a knight was combined in Don Rodrigo. . . . This remarkable man is one of the few who, eschewing all favoritism and intrigue, deceit and crime, have attained to the level of kings and been, in their own lifetime, their country's pride."

This rosy view of El Cid could not survive the scientific spirit that swept the western world with the completion of the Industrial Revolution. In 1849, a Dutch scholar named Reinhardt Dozy examined all the documents relating to El Cid, especially the Arabic sources. In keeping with the unromantic attitude of his day, Dozy blasted El Cid's legend to bits, maintaining that Spain's national hero had been little more than a soldier of fortune whose sword was available to the highest bidder.

Dozy's view was highly unpopular in Spain, but his careful scholarship made it impossible for anyone to reject his work out of hand. Finally, in 1929, Menéndez Pidal published his massive work *La España del Cid*, refuting Dozy's arguments with equally careful reference to the documents. Richly evoking the world in which El Cid performed his deeds, Menéndez Pidal restored the Castilian knight to his place of honor and glory in Spanish history. In the eyes of present-day historians such as Richard Fletcher, Menéndez Pidal's work contains flaws and exaggerations of its own. But Fletcher is quick to add, "We still think of eleventh-century Spain as the Cid's Spain, and for this we have Menéndez Pidal to thank."

Somewhat surprisingly, Hollywood did not turn its attention to the legendary warrior until 1961, when Menéndez Pidal was hired as a technical adviser for the filming of the big-budget epic *El Cid*, starring Charlton Heston as Rodrigo and Sophia Loren as Jimena. The producers went to great expense filming historically accurate battle scenes on location in Spain, and this was the true substance of the film; even the statuesque Loren, then at the height of her box-office allure, was shunted into the background while Heston repeatedly tangled with a villainous crew of Moors. (The veteran actor Herbert Lom was obliged to play Yusuf with a black mask covering most of his face.) For the end of the film, the scriptwriters drew on medieval ballads for a striking scene in which El Cid's dead body is propped up in the saddle and his horse is set off at a gallop across the battlefield, whereupon the very sight of the great warrior puts the enemy to flight. Moviegoers may not have absorbed much actual history from this, but they certainly came away with a vivid impression of Spain's national hero.

In the future, writers and scholars will undoubtedly continue to boost or diminish the image of El Cid. The final word may well belong to the 12th-century Muslim writer Ibn Bassam, who recorded with horror Rodrigo's cruelties in Valencia. Writing 10 years after Rodrigo's death, which he had no cause to regret, he granted his enemy these words of grudging admiration:

> The power of this tyrant became ever more intolerable; it weighed like a heavy load upon the people of the coast and inland regions, filling all men, both near and far, with fear. His intense ambition, his lust for power . . . caused all to tremble. Yet this man, who was the scourge of his age, was by his unflagging and clear-sighted energy, his virile character, and his heroism, a miracle among the great miracles of the Almighty.

CHRONOLOGY

Early 1040s   Born Rodrigo Díaz in Vivar, Spain

c. 1055   Becomes a squire and attends his father, Diego Laínez, in battle

1058   Diego Laínez dies; Rodrigo becomes the ward of Prince Sancho of Castile

1060   Rodrigo is knighted by King Ferdinand I of Castile

1063   Proves himself in battle for the first time, against the Aragonese, near the town of Graus in the Pyrenees Mountains

1065   King Ferdinand dies, and Sancho becomes king of Castile; Sancho names Rodrigo commander of the Castilian army; Rodrigo wins glory in single combats

1072–73   Sancho and his brother Alfonso go to war over control of Castile and León; Rodrigo does battle with 15 knights at the siege of Zamora; Sancho is killed during the siege, and his brother Alfonso becomes king; Rodrigo swears allegiance to Alfonso

1074 or 1075   Rodrigo marries Doña Jimena, daughter of the duke of Oviedo, and receives valuable properties; the couple eventually have three children, María, Cristina, and Diego

1079	Rodrigo defeats Castilians and Muslims at Cabra and holds Castilian nobles for ransom; resentful Castilians influence King Alfonso against Rodrigo
1081	Rodrigo invades territory of King Alfonso's client al-Qadir; Alfonso banishes Rodrigo; accompanied by 100 loyal knights, Rodrigo becomes a soldier of fortune
1082	Rodrigo is employed by al-Mu'tamin, the Muslim king of Zaragoza; defeats Christian troops at Tamarite de Litera, Monzón, and Almenar
1083–85	Ravages the territory of al-Mu'tamin's enemies, enriching himself with plunder and tribute
1086	Almoravids invade southern Spain from North Africa; Muslim forces under Yusuf defeat Alfonso's Castilian army at Sagrajas on October 23; Yusuf withdraws to Africa, but Alfonso comes to terms with Rodrigo
1089	Yusuf returns to Spain; Rodrigo's enemies at court influence Alfonso against him; the king banishes Rodrigo for the second time; Rodrigo defeats the count of Barcelona at Tévar
1090–93	Rodrigo establishes control of the southeastern coast of Spain; besieges Valencia after it falls to pro-Almoravid faction
1094	Conquers Valencia in May; defeats Yusuf and the Almoravids at Cuarte in October
1095–99	Rules Valencia with an iron hand, amassing great wealth and living in splendor; marries his daughters to high-ranking noblemen

1099   Dies peacefully in Valencia

1102   Doña Jimena abandons Valencia to the Muslims;
            transports the body of El Cid to his native
            Castile, where it is reburied at San Pedro de
            Cardeña

1116   Doña Jimena dies and is buried alongside her
            husband; end of the historical record of El Cid
            and his family

FURTHER READING

Bloch, Marc. *Feudal Society*. 2 Vols. Trans. L. A. Manyon. Chicago: University of Chicago Press, 1961.

Chejne, Anwar. *Muslim Spain: Its History and Culture*. Minneapolis: University of Minnesota Press, 1974.

Collins, Roger. *Early Medieval Spain: Unity in Diversity, 400–1000*. New York: St. Martin's, 1983.

Duby, Georges S. *William Marshal: The Flower of Chivalry*. Trans. Richard Howard. New York: Pantheon, 1985.

Fletcher, Richard. *The Quest for El Cid*. New York: Knopf, 1990.

Keay, S. J. *Roman Spain*. London: British Museum Publications, 1988.

Keegan, John. *The Face of Battle*. New York: Military Heritage Press, 1986.

Mackay, Angus. *Spain in the Middle Ages: From Frontier to Empire, 1000–1500*. London: Cambridge University Press, 1977.

Menéndez Pidal, Ramón. *The Cid and His Spain*. Trans. Harold Sunderland. London: John Murray, 1934.

Pirenne, Henri. *Economic and Social History of Medieval Europe*. Trans. I. E. Clegg. San Diego: Harcourt Brace Jovanovich, 1937.

The Poem of the Cid. Trans. Rita Hamilton and Janet Perry. New York: Viking Penguin, 1984.

Previté-Orton, C. W. *The Shorter Cambridge Medieval History*. 2 Vols. Cambridge: University of Cambridge Press, 1952.

INDEX

PHILIP KOSLOW is a New York–based writer and editor with a wide-ranging interest in history and literature. The editor of numerous young adult books, he is also the author of *The Securities and Exchange Commission* in the Chelsea House KNOW YOUR GOVERNMENT series.

RODOLFO CARDONA is professor of Spanish and comparative literature at Boston University. A renowned scholar, he has written many works of criticism, including *Ramón, a Study of Gómez de la Serna and His Works* and *Visión del esperpento: Teoría y práctica del esperpento en Valle-Inclán*. Born in San José, Costa Rica, he earned his B.A. and M.A. from Louisiana State University and received a Ph.D. from the University of Washington. He has taught at Case Western Reserve University, the University of Pittsburgh, the University of Texas at Austin, the University of New Mexico, and Harvard University.

JAMES COCKCROFT is currently a visiting professor of Latin American and Caribbean studies at the State University of New York at Albany. A three-time Fulbright scholar, he earned a Ph.D. from Stanford University and has taught at the University of Massachusetts, the University of Vermont, and the University of Connecticut. He is the author or coauthor of numerous books on Latin American subjects, including *Neighbors in Turmoil: Latin America*, *The Hispanic Experience in the United States: Contemporary Issues and Perspectives*, and *Outlaws in the Promised Land: Mexican Immigrant Workers and America's Future*.